Connecting to God

Nurturing Spirituality through Small Groups

Corinne Ware

An Alban Institute Publication

Library of Congress Catalog Number 97-73920
ISBN 1-56699-183-8

To

Rev. William E. Denham, Jr., Ph.D.

my friend, counselor, and first spiritual director

and to

The dean and faculty

of
The Episcopal Theological Seminary of the Southwest
whose inclusion of mystical and ascetical theology
introduced me to the study of spirituality

You would not find out the boundaries of the soul,
even by travelling along every path; so deep a measure
does it have.
Heraclitus

Whether you like it or not, whether you know it or not,
secretly nature seeks, hunts, tries to ferret out the track
on which God may be found.
Meister Johannes Eckhart

CONTENTS

FOREWORD

The issue addressed by this book, how to connect to God, is a personal issue for me. In fact, it is the most constant and consistent issue of my adult life.

I faced the issue as a youth and as a young adult. How can I be open to what God wants to do with me?

After deciding to enter the professional ministry as an ordained clergyman, I turned my attention to the church—how to lead it, how to help it grow and be strong and vital. But the question was still there. In those moments when I was able to stand apart from the church and my role as pastor and face the harsh reality that maybe I was not paying attention to the most important things, there was that same issue: *How do I direct the activities of the church toward the transforming power of God?*

In my own life (and in the lives of all those who are in my keeping), I wonder how we keep the risen Christ at the center. This issue stays with me, although sometimes it is just beneath the surface.

Corinne Ware has helped me clarify the issue and hold it front and center long enough to cause me to have to deal with it. She did so first in *Discover Your Spiritual Type* (The Alban Institute, 1995). I wore out my copy as I sought deeper understanding. Then I used the book with scores of leaders all across my denomination and beyond.

I then read *Connecting to God: Nurturing Spirituality through Small Groups* in an early draft. I knew immediately that God had sent Corinne Ware and her book to me. Now as a published work, through The Alban Institute, the book is available to a wide audience.

The issue is not how to *do church*; it is how to *love God*. It is not even how to have vital, exciting church life. It is how to keep church life focused on the One who loves us unfailingly and never lets us go.

Oh God, I want to do that! Oh God, help me do that! Help me help others do that.

As I write this foreword, I am on an extended visit with church leaders in Central America and the Caribbean. On this particular day, I am in North America, looking across a huge people-built waterway to South America. What an engineering and construction accomplishment! After several unsuccessful attempts in the nineteenth century, workers completed the Panama Canal in 1914. It was the beginning of a century of one marvel after another.

We have come to expect those marvels. We sometimes call them "miracles." People keep attempting the impossible. Humans do great things, but only God works miracles. God works miracles every day in small and in large ways. We may not even notice.

That is why Corinne Ware wrote this book—to help people pay attention to what God pays attention. In simple but powerful words, Ware says to the church:

- You can help people create settings (often in small groups) for seeking God, staying open to God, and being accountable to God.

- You can practice the spiritual disciplines that become means of grace as they help us be open to God.

- You can center on God and discover power and energy for being the people of God.

In Central America and the Caribbean, in Africa and Asia, in Europe, and all over the world, people are yearning in the deepest recesses of their beings for God. They yearn to experience God's transforming and healing grace, to live lovingly and justly with others, and to make their own lives meaningful, fruitful, and godly.

Our churches, not all, but many of them (the ones Ware addresses in this book) want to respond helpfully. But our church organization and administration, our inability to stay centered on Christ (rather than on the church), our reluctance to listen to people and to trust them to tell us what they want for their lives, and even our good works get in the way. We let our belief in our own human power usurp the place of God in our lives.

That will be a lot harder to do after reading this book. I recommend it highly not only because it is a good and worthy book, but also because it addresses the deepest struggles of my own life.

Ezra Earl Jones

PREFACE

Any "helpful" book is written because the writer believes there is some problem that needs remedy. This assumption presupposes a particular reader, one who just might want to do something about whatever that problem is.

The problem addressed by this book is this: As Christians we would like to claim for ourselves the deep spirituality that is promised by our faith, but we somehow do not have a handle on how to achieve that deeper spiritual life. Because of the accounts we have heard from other Christians, we believe this depth and spiritual dimension to be a rightful inheritance of the faith we hold. And yet it may seem to us that the spiritual dimension is a hidden mystery that does not automatically come as a result of loyalty to church, sustained activity, and moral behavior. We would like to "be spiritual" but we don't know how!

This book will attempt to solve the dilemma in two ways. First, it will provide an easily implemented model for developing spiritual life through the interaction of a small group. Second, it supplies a representative bibliography, found in the text and the endnotes, so that anyone who cares to may further investigate each of the growth-enhancing disciplines or topics suggested.

The emphasis here is on solutions that are more vertical than horizontal, which is to say the book focuses more on developing the interior life than on emphasizing numerical church growth. The spiritual formation groups discussed often become the underpinning for increased membership, but the focus of this book is on a deepened spirituality, wherever that may lead.

To Whom It May Concern

This is a book addressed to two groups: church leaders, lay and ordained, and the personnel of pastoral counseling centers. That description covers a wide spectrum, so let me qualify further to say that I am writing for all those who want to provide the "something more" they sense is possible in the Christian life. These might be in any of four categories.

First, there is the leader of a mainline Protestant church. This church may find, to its dismay, that its building is larger than is now needed for a dwindling congregation. There are more funerals held than baptisms. Each year the budget decreases. Members feel a lack of congregational vitality and discuss the need to give people more of what they want. But many flounder in their attempts to provide a deeper spiritual life, though they suspect that to be the real task of their church.

The second reader is from a more vital mainline church as described by Nancy Ammerman in her book, *Congregation and Community: Stability and Change in American Religion,*[1] or perhaps an evangelical congregation. Ammerman has discovered that there is life in mainline Protestantism, and that it is a myth to say that all such churches are declining. Some of these churches are not so "mainline" anymore, but are increasingly outside the mainstream of denominationalism. Critics describe them as being less "theologically correct," but these churches are nonetheless experiencing renewal. Some have a strong evangelical orientation and a few are among the new megachurches. Readers from these congregations could be saying, "We've got a good thing going here, but how do we grow in depth as well as in numbers?" There is no lack of spiritual experience in these churches, but there may be a desire among some of the members to tap into a lost heritage, and delve the deeper dimensions of faith. There is the lurking fear that spiritual experiences can become shallow emotionality if not stabilized by growth and grounding.

The third reader is Roman Catholic, and, because of that rich tradition, may be more aware than others of the spiritual life that is promised by Christianity. Catholics may suspect that a broader experience is there for them in prayer, study, and sharing of the faith journey. They would enjoy studying the works of their own Catholic writers, including the Christian mystics, as well as discovering the riches found in Protestantism and other Christian traditions. But Catholic readers may feel that such a life has been reserved for those trained for the priesthood or for laypeople committed to religious vocations lived in community. The Roman Catholic lay member often wonders whether growth in spirituality can be a part of "the secular life" as well as it is for those with religious vocations.

The fourth reader is on the staff of a pastoral counseling center that offers psychotherapy but with a faith perspective. I know this person; I work with pastoral counselors and I am one. We entered the field of *pastoral* counseling, not just counseling, because we understand that healing comes from both the insights of psychology and the gifts of faith. To qualify for insurance and to be reputable among mental health care peers, many pastoral counselors have emphasized the psychological skills while placing less focus on the faith dimension. Increasingly they face a critical question: How can a counseling center encourage the client's option to grow in faith without manipulating or imposing? Group work is a good solution for those wanting to offer the spiritual dimension without seeming to cram it down people's throats. Joining a group should always be the choice of the client, who would join in response to the group's purposes. A group focused on spiritual growth would be selected by the client because of the group's content, not because the counselor insisted such a perspective was necessary.

A pastoral counseling center is the logical setting for training clients and churches in the skills for spiritual development. I trust that in this book pastoral counselors will find a format for starting a group specifically designed for their clients seeking spiritual growth. Although most of what is presented here is couched in language addressed to church leaders, almost all of it is applicable to pastoral counselors. The group is not presented as a therapy group, but rather is growth oriented. I encourage pastoral psychotherapists to interpret and adapt this material in a way that is to their advantage in their own settings.

What Lies Ahead

We are about to consider a new model for spiritual growth: the spiritual formation group. Chapter 1 is an introduction exploring what spirituality is and is not, discussing the goals of this group approach to developing spirituality, and the advantages of this project being a lay-led ministry.

Chapter 2 examines "why in groups?" rather than in the more traditional format of individual spiritual direction. This includes a brief history of methods used in the past to foster spiritual formation, beginning with Hebrew practices, the New Testament mentoring style, and continuing to the present, and an evaluation of advantages and disadvantages of using the group format.

Chapter 3 presents concrete plans for beginning and structuring a spiritual formation group. Suggestions are given for the first meeting and for helping participants to clarify what they need from the experience. I lay out a secure framework so that the group can easily get through its first months.

Chapters 4 through 7 are the heart of the book and offer specific suggestions for the activities of the group: prayer, study, sharing, and a rule. These four chapters make it easy for the convener to guide the group time in ways that are engaging and challenging. I list plenty of tools so the convener need not worry about "what next?" Readers are encouraged to seek their own variations as the group begins to form its unique identity and discern its own needs.

Chapter 8 describes who may be best suited as conveners and discusses some other practical decisions that can help ensure the group's success. The chapter includes a discussion of accountability, safeguards needed to prevent the group from getting off track, and possible abuses that can occur and ways to deal with them.

Chapter 9 gives suggestions for the aftercare of those who leave the group, and comments on what may happen for group members and for the church at large because of the presence of a vital, ongoing spiritual formation group.

To the reader: I wish you well as you consider the possibilities of what may take place when you initiate this plan for spiritual growth. As you progress in the book, I think you will know if a spiritual growth group is for you. Take time to think through adapting what is presented to fit your own situation.

Remember that you are not in charge of the outcome of your group venture. God's spirit is the actual director, and your part is to respond in ways that best enhance spiritual growth for you and in others. Join me as we discuss the ways to do exactly that, using a spiritual formation group model.

ACKNOWLEDGMENTS

My chief thanks go to those teachers along the way who have introduced me to the history of spirituality and to the application of its disciplines. Gratitude also to the friends who have read parts of the manuscript for this book and made always helpful suggestions. Rev. Krista Kiger, a creative Presbyterian pastor, has been one of these. I am indebted to Dr. Ezra Earl Jones, general secretary to The General Board of Discipleship, The United Methodist Church, for his support of my work and his interest in making this book as good as it could be. He put me in touch with Rev. Dick Wills, pastor of Christ Church, United Methodist, in Fort Lauderdale, whose enthusiasm and powerful story have influenced my thinking as to how group work can empower churches.

I am indebted to Sr. Agnes Honz, OSB, who generously provided the videotapes by Thomas Keating as well as other resources from the library at Mount Saint Scholastica Benedictine Convent in Atchison, Kansas. Thanks to Sr. Mary Teresa Morris, OSB, also of Mount Saint Scholastica Convent, who obtained for me books and references on the history and spirituality of the Benedictine order. I value the friendship of both of these fine women. Another friend, Rabbi Matt Friedman of Temple Adath Joseph, St. Joseph, Missouri, has helped with the translation of a Hebrew word and its occurrence in the Reformed liturgy.

Being able to pick up the telephone and ask a former professor about a book or opinion related to his field of expertise is a luxury I thoroughly appreciate. My thanks to Prof. Jon Rainbow of Southern Baptist Theological Seminary in Louisville, Kentucky, for his suggestions about group leadership, and for my experience in his course on group dynamics. Thanks also to Dr. William Pitts, professor of history in the Department of Religion, Baylor University, for his friendship as well as his

Rolodex mind, being able to instantly tell me what book I might need for a particular purpose.

Celia Allison Hahn, recent past editor in chief of The Alban Institute, has been consistently supportive, encouraging me ever so gently to persist in this project. Alban authors have been fortunate to have her on their side. I wish her well in her new adventures. Chris Conner has carried the book through the publishing process in Celia's absence, and I appreciate both her kindness and diligence. Particular gratitude is due editor Evelyn Bence, who has added immeasurably to the quality of this work. She improved my style and enriched the content. And I am grateful to my friend Julie Buzbee, who came to the rescue with an acceptable book title.

I am grateful to Menninger Clinic, Topeka, Kansas, for their excellent study workshops offered to professional clinical therapists. Their belief that spirituality is an essential part of mental health has reinforced my own conviction that the integration of these two fields is both natural and necessary.

Finally, my thanks go to the friends, familiar and new, who expressed approval and enthusiasm for my first book, *Discover Your Spiritual Type* (Alban, 1995). It has been gratifying to hear from graduate students writing papers based on the typology, from clergy, lay leaders, and searchers of all kinds who are clearly committed to developing and deepening the spiritual as a dimension of contemporary life. Such response provides encouragement to write again.

CHAPTER 1

Do I Really Want to "Be Spiritual"?

The death of religion comes with the repression of the high hope of adventure.

Alfred North Whitehead

I am particularly struck by a metaphor used by the Quaker writer Elton Trueblood. During the fifties and early sixties it seemed that almost every year he came out with a small but insightful book. During that time he called us "the cut flower generation," by which he meant that we, especially the church, were like a flower in full bloom that had been cut at the stem; we were severed from our tap root. Indeed, in that generation churches did bloom, so to speak. The sixties was a decade of flourishing growth and of high activity. Looking back on Trueblood's analysis, we see that we are experiencing the withering of what we call mainline churches. What do you suppose happened? Did we cut ourselves off from our nutrient source, spiritual energy exhausted, as the busy church wilted? If that's the case, how can we begin to reconnect to that source again? That is the concern of this book.

The Popularity of Things Spiritual

We are definitely experiencing a sea change. Have you noticed the religion section in your local chain bookstore? No doubt there are several shelves entirely devoted to books on spirituality. And if you browse through book catalogs and religion book lists coming in the mail, you'll note a new trend. Ten years ago the banners at the top of the page announcing book categories might have included "theology," "biblical studies," perhaps "self help." But not "spirituality." Now most catalogs devote not just one but several pages in each issue to spirituality. And who would have predicted that Thomas Moore's book *Care of the Soul*, published in 1992, would remain on the best-seller list for so long? Quite suddenly we have decided that our souls have become important enough to care for.

And what of our obsession with angels? Recent television shows have featured interviews with people who claim to have seen angels or crossed paths with them in some manner. There is a proliferation of books about angels. And women can be seen wearing angel earrings, one flying in from each side.

Lately everyone seems to be talking "spirituality," and it has become religiously correct to say you are into it. We are almost sure we need more of it, but are not quite sure what "it" is.

What Is Spirituality?

Some churchgoers worry that spirituality is a New Age religion, while others think of it as being contained chiefly within Roman Catholic monastic life. But the spiritual is more than a trend or a location. It involves the God-shaped space found in the inmost part of each human being. The spiritual nature of our being has always been part of us.

My definition of *spirituality* is simply "connecting to God." That may seem too simple, but give it a chance; let it sink in. By somehow responding to the Creator, by sensing that we are accompanied, we feel a quite different dimension in our lives. We have all had moments when we felt this extraordinary sense of having connected to something larger than ourselves. The problem to be solved, both by individual people and by congregations, is how to nurture that sense of connection. We know from experience that we cannot command it. How does a person or a group develop and increase capacity to experience God? We imagine there must be some magical way. This seems to be a mystery that we in the West do not know how to approach.

An important thing to remember is that our own efforts do not produce the God connection. We do not bring God to us by means of something we achieve, as un-American as that sounds. We can only experience the God who is *already here.* Our efforts, then, are to enhance openness and availability. Spirituality is deepened by access. It is not God who is unavailable. It is you and I.

It has been popular, in talking about spiritual growth, to speak of "making a place for God." If by that we mean giving importance to God in our lives, it is an acceptable phrase. But this can take on false overtones. The statement can imply that God is not already in every place. In learning how to "be spiritual," our task is to position ourselves so that we can hear the voice that always speaks, feel the nearness of the always present Presence, and speak to One who continually hears.

Curse and Blessing

What effect does the popularity of "spirituality" have on us? How are we influenced by this renewed interest in interior life, much of which is foreign to our traditional modes of worship and our goal-oriented way of looking at things? The results, I think, are mixed. There is both curse and blessing in this fascination with the spiritual.

The negative effect is that the popularity of spirituality can serve to trivialize our deepest feelings. Some of us have treasured a deep spiritual life long before it was discovered by aficionados of the spiritual growth movements. For a long time now we may have valued that inner part of ourselves that was connecting us to something higher and stronger than ourselves. We may feel put off by this sudden interest in spirituality and wish to have nothing to do with it. Indeed, we may sense that as people of faith, we have been made laughable to more erudite types. We also fear the effects on those among us who suffer insecurity and will grasp at any magic.

The current interest in things spiritual has also had a disorienting effect as we experience a shift in society's perception of what constitutes reality. Until recently the culture has not resonated to the unseen. Karen Armstrong, in her book *A History of God,* reminds us of what we have believed throughout the twentieth century.

> One of the reasons why religion seems irrelevant today is that many of us no longer have the sense that we are surrounded by the unseen. Our scientific culture educates us to focus our attention on the physical and material world in front of us. This method of looking at the

world has achieved great results. One of its consequences, however, is that we have, as it were, edited out the sense of the "spiritual" or the "holy" which pervades the lives of people in more traditional societies at every level and which was once an essential component of our human experience of the world.[1]

While a scientific culture has historically educated us to focus on the material world, later individual scientists, from Teilhard de Chardin to some of today's quantum physicists, have been in the vanguard, leading us back into the world of creation and mystery. It is often the scientist who reports experiencing the transcendent. Many people find themselves confused by this transition as they move from a world view that has not given credence to the unprovable to one that allows for the transcendent. We are coming to see, along with Armstrong, that "throughout history, men and women have experienced a dimension of spirit that seems to transcend the mundane world."[2] We have always been spiritual creatures, and one would have to work very hard to kill the tendency.

There is a plus side to the popularity of spirituality, however. We are at last being offered hope that this deepest part of ourselves is being acknowledged. Others are giving consideration to the possibility of the "something more" that we have suspected was there all along. Many are silently saying, "Now people will know why this part of life is so important to me; I am not weird!"

Risks and Fears

I think church leaders can see the risks involved if worshippers seriously position themselves to hear God's voice. Uncontrolled influence is the corporate risk. Were they to become more connected to God, and were they to feel more acutely God's participation in their lives, what might they be led to think and do? Could they be "controlled"? Consider a worst case scenario: Might someone hear God saying the local church should be shut down? Probably not. More likely someone would be impressed with something like "Feed my sheep," or "Inasmuch as you have done it to the least of these, you have done it to me."

There is also the individual risk, one that reflects a person's fear of what it would mean to listen to God. What if I go off the deep end? And what, one wonders, would God "do to me" were I to be in the presence of the Holy? The fundamental question is whether one is safe to truly risk cooperating with God in the world and in one's individual life. I particularly like a phrase used by Gustavo Gutierrez when he describes spirituality as "walking in freedom."[3] Freedom is always scary!

Spiritual Formation in a Group Setting

If the risk of openness to God is deemed to be worth the effort, then how is a person or group to grow in relationship to God? How is spirituality developed?

I do not believe that inattention to the inner life happens because people are, at heart, unwilling. I think the unfamiliar territory makes us skittish. If I had grown up in a religious tradition that stressed quietness and inner listening, further developing that skill would seem no great mystery to me. I would have some familiarity with how to value and attend to that part of my life.

If, however, I grew up in a church setting that valued "showing up," being involved in activities, contributing time, energy, and financial resources, I would know how to do those things especially well. Most congregations do a better job of organizing committees, carrying out activities, and having potlucks than they do of deepening spiritual life. (Of course many of these activities have great value for the community and in their own way foster spiritual life as they carry out the values of faith.) Church members in the United States, Protestants in particular, know how to organize and get things done. We do it better than anybody. We also like to use words and we do that well. So when spirituality is mentioned, and we think of waiting and listening, not doing and speaking, it throws us. This is not what we do!

There is a solution. The Western church tradition stresses the coming together of like-minded people to make decisions, to study, to plan, and to act. In other words, *we function effectively in groups*. We learn about groups in grade school (were you a Red Bird or a Yellow Wren?), and we are trained toward cooperative efforts in sports, civic, and business organizations. We know how to use the gifts of the many to contribute to a common good. You might call it training in democracy. We watch the chaos in countries conducting their first political elections and are puzzled when they don't know exactly how to pull it off.

We know how to work in groups, but we also like to be autonomous, so autonomous that what is traditionally called "spiritual direction" is not a part of the Protestant tradition. Protestants, whose history is one of individualism, are reluctant to be "directed" by anyone! Americans in particular are wary of being overcontrolled by others, and the word *direction* implies to us a loss of freedom.

And yet today there is a renewed interest in learning the disciplines of spiritual formation and receiving the gifts of spiritual direction. Because of our training in group processes and obsession with autonomy, we just might enjoy engaging in spiritual formation within self-directing groups. I propose that traditions that typically use groups of people to carry on the work of the church will more easily move into spiritual formation ideas if they are presented in a group format. The specific ways in which group study and experience differ from individual experience will be discussed in a later chapter.

Goals and Objectives

Goals of the Book

The first purpose of this book is to present a model for facilitating spiritual formation, or spiritual growth, using a group rather than the individual "direction," approach. Working with a group is different! Some people accustomed to individual spiritual formation patterns may doubt the value of using group work for spiritual development. It is true that something of individual direction is lost in the translation. It is also true that *something is gained*, and a group can provide unique experiences and insights not possible in any other approach.

A second goal of this book is to allay a facilitator's fears as to how the spiritual formation group will be conducted. A concrete plan is given providing a structure for beginning and conducting the group. This can easily be changed as the group gets a feel for this type of activity and begins to set its own agenda. A spiritual formation group may like this structure so well that it continues to use it, or the group may make adjustments as the needs of the group change.

The important third goal is in helping lay church members accept responsibility for their spiritual growth. As long as we depend on others to make us spiritually open, we will fail. Competent clergy know this better than anyone, and there is much despair among them at those moments when they know very well that they are expected to be the spiritual "hired hand" for others.

Objectives for the Group

The first objective of the group is to create an atmosphere for listening, a climate in which members can hear the call of God in their lives. Most Christians believe in "calling" but confine its application to ordained clergy. A calling is that particular pull of God on us, any of us, to do some particular thing. To hear this call, one must first be able to listen. A group focused on spiritual growth will be an oasis for those who wonder if they are being guided into some particular work or interest. They will have new material to think about individually, and they will be able to test their feelings as they interact in the group.

Feedback from members may reveal any number of vocations within the group. We may come to realize we have gifts we did not suspect were there. It is amazing how many laypeople are called to the spiritual direction of others. The historical record tells us that this was as true in the early church and in medieval times as it is today. The spiritual formation group is a healthy environment in which the convener, or any other member who feels he or she may be called to this work, can test that vocation. The group will provide the response that affirms the vocation or says instead, "Wait and reconsider." In a group one can assess his or her ability to respond intuitively to others and discern a path for growth.

The second concern of the spiritual formation group is to serve as a safeguard. Now that spirituality has become popular, many people are rushing into the subject, swallowing whole everything that is published or televised. A spiritual growth group provides a realistic context in which seekers can discuss and get feedback about the new ideas they encounter.

Finally, the third objective for the group is to create a community of people whose task is to accompany, not persuade. I do not trust or believe in coercive religion. Persuasion is God's business. Being "a friend alongside" is ours. After all, what do we really know of another person's history or hidden needs? We may think we know what those needs are bound to be, but that kind of assumption can be deadly. If we really do believe that one of God's manifestations among us is God's Spirit, then we may trust the Spirit to guide and persuade. Our part is to be present to others in their journey and allow them to accompany us in ours.

Empowering a Lay-Led Ministry

This section is addressed especially to the clergyperson who may be considering beginning a group for spiritual formation within his or her church. As you know, there are certain things that trained clergy do best, and many are skilled in the work of spiritual formation. But I would like to suggest that the spiritual formation group be a lay-member project. Group leadership seems particularly adaptable to the gifts laypeople bring to the church, and the group will more likely flourish if leadership comes from grassroots rather than if it is handed down or directed by a church official. This does not imply that the spiritual formation group is a lone ranger out there, answering to no one. In chapter 8 we will discuss the issue of accountability. Any cleric leader will rightly oppose a "church within the church" aberration. On the other hand, skillful clergy see their calling as that of enabling others to grow. Like the apostle Paul, their work is to "equip the saints" for the work of ministry. There is a necessary balance between the clergyperson's connection to the group and his or her allowing it to function as a lay endeavor.

There are probably some laypeople in your congregation who have been wanting just such an in-depth experience of greater spiritual development. Somewhere in the course of mid-adult life people tend to get tired of busyness and of climbing the ladder. *Is this all there is?* they wonder. They look to their worship experience for the something more they seek. Such people, whatever their ages, are the laymen and laywomen among whom you will find members and leadership for the spiritual formation group. In a survey done by Trinity Church, New York, 80 percent of respondents stated that the thing they most needed from their congregations was spiritual formation.[4] As Charles Colson says, in the United States Christianity is "3,000 miles wide and half an inch deep."[5] There are some in the church who say, "But I want to go deeper!"

So long as laypeople expect pastors and priests to seek God in their stead and make no effort of their own, they will be disappointed and stunted. Many clergy yearn for the power and vitality generated by lay members who refresh the congregation with a contagious spirituality born of study and prayer and a lively faith. Such church leaders are eager to empower laypeople to engage in their own spiritual development.

So there just may be a way to engage in a deeper spirituality, even in our current accelerated technological society. Developing one's spirituality need not be limited to approaches used in the past. Let us now explore the reasons for thinking that spiritual growth just might be fostered in a contemporary group setting.

CHAPTER 2

Spiritual Formation: Individual and Group Approaches

For the avoidance of error, have someone to advise you—a spiritual father or confessor, a brother of like mind; and make known to him all that happens to you in the work of prayer.

Theophan the Recluse

The skill of offering spiritual guidance to others has always been a mentoring project, whether it is one person who is being guided or a group of people. A mentor is one who serves as a trusted counselor or teacher, one who safely guides toward the chosen destination. The goal of the spiritual mentor has been to foster in others the development of *a personal consciousness of divinity*. That statement would probably be true for any major religion; it is certainly so of Christianity.

Claiming Our Inheritance

When I first gained an interest in the study of spirituality, I was astonished at my ignorance about those who had preceded me in the faith. I discovered centuries of writings by people who had hard-won insights about prayer and the ups and downs of spiritual life. It was like looking at a genealogy and discovering that you are a direct descendent of some notable person. I had the feeling that must come to an adopted child when she has just been told about her birth parents. One of the things I learned about my heritage was that these spiritual ancestors had made a vigorous and intentional effort to grow toward God. They had sought teachers, spent time in silent retreats, and had gathered with like-minded seekers. Whether they were alone, with one other person, or participating in groups, they had done whatever they could to grow!

Let us look to our own Christian history and claim the inheritance of a spiritual tradition passed down to us but often covered over, even lost, in our own religious experience. Whether we accomplish our spiritual growth through one-on-one mentoring or by being nurtured in a group of fellow seekers, it is important that we discover the Christian spiritual legacy left by centuries of practicing Christians, making it our own. The premise of this book is that with the encouragement provided by a group, we may be more likely to seek out and reclaim our rightful spiritual history.

The Legacy of Scripture

The biblical legacy is the one most familiar to us, and it testifies to the importance of growing and maintaining our connection with God. The Hebrew scriptures are filled with powerful figures who arrive on the scene just as the people need a word from God or a reminder that humankind, if it is to flourish, must be responsive to God. The Hebrew prophets always warned that becoming distant from God had dire consequences. Very often their counsel was effective in mentoring the people back toward their holy calling. The psalmists' religion celebrated this loving response to God as being not only a duty but a good and joyful thing. Waiting for God is the persistent theme, as in Psalm 62:5: "My soul, wait in silence for God only, / For my hope is from Him." This "waiting" was done for a God who comes and relates personally, a Hebrew concept that would later become central to Christian faith.

According to the gospels, one of Jesus' gifts was to mentor, that is, to convey to those around him the centrality of being in touch with God. He went about living and teaching that message. Nicodemus observed, "Rabbi, we know that You have come from God as a teacher; for no one can do these signs that You do unless God is with him" (John 3:2). Harnack claimed "Jesus sought to kindle independent religious life, and he did kindle it; yes, that is his peculiar greatness, that he led men to God so that they lived their own life with Him."[1]

The Early Church Pattern

Members of the early church mentored one another in the faith and, from the first, understood themselves as being community, a mode of thinking that was a direct outgrowth of an Old Testament mind set. As a consequence of this Jewish parentage, early church spirituality was marked by a strong sense of communal connection with God and the deep belief that an individual could be personally connected to God. Spiritual formation took place informally within the close-knit *koinonia* of early church believers. A coherent theology had not yet been worked out, and certainly there was no formalized "path" toward spiritual growth. That was to come later and in many forms. For early Christians, growth took place in their association with one another. It is no wonder that sharing a meal together came to be called *communion*, communion with God and with one another.

In the fourth century, those we call the Desert Fathers sought simplicity and a single-minded focus on God; they settled in the Egyptian desert, or other remote places, to achieve the solitude they needed. The interesting thing to notice about these early seekers is that, even in their solitude, they often lived in loosely formed groups. Some chose to be at a distance from the others, at times silent and scattered, but they were nonetheless a community. Their gift to us was their understanding of the value of individual inner perception and of shared experience. In their writings they remind their successors that even the solitary among us need from others accountability and companionship.

A Tradition of Spiritual Direction

What we now think of as spiritual direction, a practice known from Hebrew scripture and New Testament accounts, continues and evolves in the present. It may have earlier been called something else, or perhaps called nothing at all, but we see clear historical evidence of one person mentoring another in that person's spiritual journey. Prominent examples of individual mentoring are the relationships of Elijah to Elisha and of the apostle Paul to his young friend Timothy. Paul's writing to Timothy is full of advice, warnings, and directions on every topic, which may be one reason we call it *direction*. Today we are more inclined to favor the concept of *companionship-in-the-journey*. This egalitarian approach is more comfortable to members of a democratic and individualistic society. In fact, many dislike the term *direction,* preferring words such as *guide* or *spiritual friend.* I agree with this preference, but because *spiritual direction* is the more familiar term, it will be the one most often used here, along with the word *mentor,* which is apropos to our meaning.

As methods of spiritual formation evolved, they became increasingly characterized by discipline. The Rule of Saint Benedict, as well as numerous other "paths" in the spiritual life, developed as a way to discipline daily life toward holiness. The medieval mystics devised various spiritual *ladders* by which one could climb to reach God in a closer way. These ladders were seen as an arduous ascent toward God, one which often required ascetic practices such as fasting, sleeplessness, and the rigorous structuring of daily time. The mystics exhibited an amazing dedication to live out these disciplined methods of achieving holiness. Our legacy includes valuable personal accounts written in the Middle Ages by people of faith.

The Celtic church in Britain continued the mentoring tradition calling the spiritual director "soul friend," a phrase appropriated by Kenneth Leech for the title of his excellent book on spiritual direction.[2] While fourth-century Celtic spiritual mentoring stressed mutuality and support, the twelfth-century Cistercian tradition brought to full flower the requirement of obedience to one's spiritual guide. To this, Aelred added friendship as an important component of effective spiritual companionship.

Manuals and books about spiritual direction proliferated throughout the twelfth to fourteenth centuries. Thirteenth-century laypeople, both women and men, were often consulted as directors. Julian of Norwich is one of the more famous female spiritual directors; because of their writings left to us, we now know about many others.

Some Contemporary Developments

In more recent times a great amount of writing was done by Anglicans and other Protestants. While the sermon was stressed as a source of spiritual instruction, it was assumed that believers would also seek out personal guidance. The Anglican tradition of spiritual guidance has continued in the more contemporary works of Evelyn Underhill, H. S. Box, and, more recently, Martin Thornton and Kenneth Leech.

In England and in the United States there is now a great interest in the blending of spiritual formation with the insights of psychology. It is not uncommon to find Episcopal priests who are also Jungian analysts. One evidence of the confluence of religion and psychology, which began in Protestant life and quickly became a part of all major faith groups, is the emergence of what is called pastoral counseling, which is seen as both a pastoral skill and as a profession within psychotherapy.

Today spirituality is again being seen as a suitable pursuit for group work. The formation of groups focused on mutual support and the training of members is a prominent feature of our culture. We create groups to study just about everything and to share our similar stories. Groups gathered for the express purpose of spiritual growth and inquiry are also appearing, and some of the better models for these are seen in churches.

Types of Groups

It can be rightly claimed that churches already have more than enough groups of various kinds. But most church groups are formed either for increased numerical growth or for more effective pastoral care. Groups interested in numerical growth have as their goal the enlistment of others into the community of faith. Groups formed for pastoral care are created as minipastorates for developing community and care of a large congregation that cannot be fully attended to by clergy. These groups typically provide fellowship, Bible study, and service activities. One church with an extraordinary group program along this caring model is Christ Church, United Methodist, in Fort Lauderdale, Florida. They began with sixteen groups and after four years have seventy. A "leader" recruits the members, between six and fourteen; they meet once a week to pray, study scripture or something scripture related, and to share their lives. These groups also commit to some outreach project of their choosing. In describing this movement within the church, their pastor, Dick Wills, said "There is just this incredible joy, a vitality that feeds everything else." If you are interested in more about this group model, read Wills's article in the April 1995 issue of *Circuit Rider*, a United Methodist publication.[3] If using groups primarily for caring and church growth is what most interests you, look also into the publications by the Vineyard Group, a nondenominational organization that has manuals for training group leaders as well as group members.[4]

As you see, groups designed to meet congregational needs have existed in the past and are now very effectively taking place in many caring communities. It is my contention, however, that a deepened spirituality is often not well attended to, even in the finest group efforts. I think the reason may be, first of all, our lack of familiarity with what we would *do* if we were to join together in such a venture. We have, after all, lost touch with so much that is part of our heritage. Second, I think we are almost afraid of what familiarity with prayer, meditation, reading of the mystics, and sharing of spiritual concerns might mean for us. There are some risks, of course. None of us grows without change and enlargement.

Reasonable Caution

Many Protestants are guarded about what has long been called spiritual direction. The Reformed tradition warns against the undue spiritual influence of anyone but Christ. The Reformers recognized and theologically guarded themselves against the perils of human fallibility, and their concern about being told what to do by a "higher"—but possibly misguided—human authority is a reasonable caution. Their alternative was to develop a pattern of mutual care that became typical among the Reformation and evangelical communities. This pattern has now become prevalent in Catholic and Episcopal churches. The group-as-minipastorate approach often works well, but sometimes the caring community can lose its original vision, forgetting the deeper spirituality that first motivated its caring actions. Because of this lost sense of purpose on the part of church members, the modern pastor, in particular, finds her- or himself called on to preach, visit, console, administrate, and generally do it all. Church members must not also expect that they "be made spiritual" by their clergy. Members might accept the pastor's or priest's encouragement and instruction to deepen their inner life, but this growth is most of all a personal, do-it-yourself effort. Leech points out that "a 'do-it-yourself' spirituality was to remain one of the central features not only of the Puritans but of wide sections of evangelical Christianity."[5]

We are correct in being wary of any who tell us that our relationship to God must be shaped exactly as they describe. On the other hand, in rejecting all help, could we be missing out on the riches that are there for us? Is pride perhaps our problem? One need not swallow everything one hears or reads, but to cast aside the gifts of others, past and present, seems critically dangerous. At the very least, deprivation will certainly keep us undernourished—underdeveloped and spiritually stunted.

Pros and Cons of Group Work

This brief history of the development of spiritual formation has told us that spiritual companionship has been done by mutually mentoring communities, by religious orders living in community, and on an individual basis. When contemporary seekers think of wanting to grow spiritually, the one-on-one form of spiritual direction is often chosen. What are the clear disadvantages and advantages of choosing the group —rather than the individual—approach to spiritual formation? Actually, they should not be compared, because they are quite different, each offering a unique advantage and diverse richness. Often a person entering individual direction will later seek out a group setting, and vice versa. One of the things we should consider at this point is the pros and cons of fostering our spiritual formation by using a group approach. One major disadvantage will be addressed, and then some important advantages explored.

One Size Does Not Fit All

We sometimes buy clothes marked "one size fits all." The advantage of individually sized clothes is that they are more likely to be an exact fit. The drawback I see to a group approach is that the group is not tailored to a specific individual's need. A group will meet the spiritual growth needs of some more than others. It is more like the difference between "tailor-made" and "one size fits all."

There is, in group work, a certain loss of personal resonance, a distinct advantage found in individual direction. A person is more intensely attended to when there are only two in the room, when that individual's words and feeling are the only subject being considered. In a nutshell, the drawback of group work is the loss of a more individualized and exclusive focus.

Enlarged through Interaction

One of the advantages of group work, one that is its special gift, is that we are made to consider several other points of view. By listening to and interacting with others, we push the boundaries of our spiritual knowledge and experience. We see things through the eyes and life events of those around us. In a word, we are enlarged!

Interaction sparks new interests and calls into question our long-held assumptions. Depend on it; someone in the group will ask how it is that we think a certain thing is true. Through interaction we become accountable and therefore more thoughtful. "Work out your own salvation" becomes a work in progress when we become part of a spiritual growth group. This quotation, taken from Paul in his letter to the Philippian church, appears in the context of Paul urging his readers to engage in the process toward wholeness. He continues by adding a promise: "For it is God who is at work within you" (2:12-13).

Safety in Numbers

Another reason for the appeal of a group is its safety. Few of us seek to go unaccompanied into the unfamiliar. If spiritual growth seems to be a risk into unknown territory, a person who may not pursue the journey individually might consider it within the context of a supportive group. As we mentioned in chapter 1, people who are not accustomed to or trained in developing inner life are often fearful of "going off the deep end." But among a trusted community of friends, they may feel comfortable, assured that if they do indeed stray into a dangerous path, someone will nudge them back and continue walking with them as they make their course correction.

Discipline and Accountability

A group provides two elements essential to spiritual growth: discipline and accountability. Consider the fact that only a few of us try to get a formal education independent of classroom demands. Those who take this route are internally motivated to do all they must do until their goals are achieved. I am not always as good at discipline as these people. I need to know that my class will meet at the appointed time, that I will need to study or prepare something in particular by a certain deadline, and that if I don't, someone will want to know why. I do some of my best work when something is required of me, that is, within a framework of discipline and accountability.

Have you ever promised yourself that you will walk a certain number of miles each day? We tend to fall by the wayside unless we have a friend who says, "I'm coming by, so be ready." The secret of Weight Watchers and of the twelve-step programs is found in the groups' support and expectations. How many people skip a dessert because they know they will be weighed-in right in front of the others? It is not that we don't want to do what we set out to do. The spirit is willing but we are easily overcome by our very human inertia. Someone waiting for us, expecting to see us and hear about our progress, can provide the extra motivation we need to keep on moving down our path.

Readers of any of the six novels in the Church of England series by Susan Howatch may have noticed her constant theme of accountability.[6] Without someone to whom they are accountable, someone who is strong enough to tell them the truth about themselves, the central characters in the stories are shown to suffer personal disaster. Their lives spiral downward until their falls are intercepted by steadying and compassionate hands. A group can provide a similar stabilizing presence and does so in a particularly effective way.

An Enriched Exchange

Another advantage of group work is that we are exposed to more information than we alone can read about. Say every group member is asked to read in an area that is then being studied by the group. When the group convenes, members discuss their own discoveries, and also hear from others who have read in material they might not have chosen. Again, all are enlarged.

Like reading and study, the experience of prayer is also enlarged by being shared in a group context. Consider how expansive it might be to experience prayer among several others. Our solitary praying melds with their intention, a very powerful thing. Groups intensify some experiences and the very presence of others changes the dynamic. (This is especially true of a group focused on spiritual growth.) It may be that in the future we will need an intentional community life more than we have ever needed it before.

Alvin Toffler, who years ago so accurately predicted our "future shock," has recently said that with the return of the worker to home and independent entrepreneurship, one common experience of future Americans will be loneliness.[7] If he is as accurate about our future as he has proved to be about our present, then deeply connecting group experiences will become more important than we may now guess. In such a society, now already upon us, we will need more than ever to attend to meaning in life, and to spirit. The dynamic in our lives is changed, not only by being with others, but by being with God, and we trust that where two or three are gathered together "in My name, there am I in their midst" (Matt. 18:20).

Attracting the Extrovert

The spiritual formation group has the advantage of attracting those who might not otherwise attend to their spiritual life on an individual basis. It is easy to forget the active extrovert when we are imagining who might be interested in spiritual growth. We think of less visible people, those who are somewhat quiet and withdrawing, as the "naturals" for spiritual pursuits. It is true that people who are seekers of the more mystical side of spirituality are often those who are somewhat interior by nature; it is their temperament. They seem to deal more easily with ideas of God's absence and God's silence. Forgotten in all this are the spiritual needs of the more sensory person and those of the extrovert. Their spirituality thrives in the context of other people!

A group mix that includes the inward and the outward, of the introvert and extrovert, is an especially rich combination for a group working

with questions of spirituality. Each has something of value to bring to
the mix, and a gathering of six or seven is likely to include both kinds
of temperament. People who are outgoing, who need interaction with
others, are always called on to head committees, participate in drives, or
organize campaigns. They are seldom considered when something like
spiritual development is involved, yet their yearning for the "something
more" can be as great as that of the more interior person. It is important
to make a place at the table for them. Groups provide that place.

The Mentoring Context

As Americans and as Christians we are well trained to function in clus-
ters. The work we do is often performed by teams, and we know all the
ropes when it comes to forming a committee, a support group, or setting
up a task force. We have a hundred different names for what are essentially groups of us. It's what we do best. We choose to be in groups
because they offer us something we cannot attain individually. The
question presented here is why one would choose to deepen spiritual life
by joining a group formed for that purpose. Some of those answers are
discussed above.

But, finally, it is important to say that because of our drift away from
the disciplines and inquiries that foster spiritual growth, we are in need
of a mentoring context, one whose intention is recovery of the spiritual.
We yearn for close and familiar companionship with God, yet, on our
own, we are at a loss as to how that might be sought. Let us claim our
inheritance! There are riches within the Christian tradition that cast light
on the path. It is worth doing. Going further in the spiritual journey is
moving toward what we are intended by our Creator to be. Working out
our salvation, to use Paul's words, is the most exciting adventure left to
us.

A Bibliographical Note

If you are interested in further study about spiritual formation through
groups, you may wish to read *Living in the Presence: Disciplines for the
Spiritual Heart* by Tilden Edwards,[8] and *Soul Feast* by Marjorie J.

Thompson.[9] Edwards's book has a section about groups, and
Thompson's book, though more valuable as an individual approach,
makes suggestions for group use. The third book I recommend is specifically designed for fostering contemplative practice in a group setting.
It is written by Gerald May and is called *Pilgrimage Home.*[10] These
writers are all fine, experienced practitioners in their fields, and their
contributions will enrich what you are considering here in this book.

CHAPTER 3

What Happens in a Spiritual Formation Group?

*. . . they wanted to be told what to do and how to do it.
But on the other hand, they did not want to be told what to
think, feel or believe.*

Gerald G. May

The insightful quotation above is taken from a very helpful book by
Gerald May; in *Pilgrimage Home*, he describes training methods developed by the Shalem Institute in Washington, D.C.[1] As May notes, what
mature seekers really want is a *way* to do things, not a set of imposed
experiences or beliefs.

If you are thinking of the spiritual formation group as being useful
in evangelizing others to a particular point of view, abandon the project.
Persuading may be exactly what is needed in your situation, but you will
be more accurate if you call that sort of approach evangelism or a course
in particular doctrines. I would urge you not to label it spiritual formation. *Spiritual formation* implies an openness to the unexpected. While
the group may have a clear format to follow, the results are unknown.
Who among us can know beyond doubt what God's Spirit will say or
will form in our life or the life of another? Within this setting we are
not managers, but observers. *Our task is to accompany, not to persuade.*

The First Meeting

The first meeting is for inquiry, not for commitment, and needs to be
informal and friendly, providing a time for inquirers to get a feel for

what this particular collection of people is like. This is the one meeting during which having more than coffee and cookies may be appropriate. The first meeting is also designed to answer questions and clarify concerns and would necessarily be different in format and purpose from the meetings that follow. (Chapter 8 will provide suggestions about forming a group, its ideal size, meeting place, leadership, and other practical matters.) At the initial gathering you could ask each one to say why he or she might want to join this kind of group. What are the participants' expectations? Because people need to know the *how-to* part, as the May quotation suggests, the convener can present a suggested outline for how the group's time will be spent. A proposed plan is given below. It is important to remain flexible and not absolutely wedded to the plan. Equally important, however, is watching for objections that are based on fear of the unfamiliar.

Establishing Trust

An example of this fear of the unfamiliar can be seen when we introduce the word *meditation*. Some hearers are pleased at the prospect of learning more about it. Others may feel that being taught meditation skills would be bootlegging New Age ideas or an Eastern religion into their church; they might object, not knowing what you mean by the word *meditation*. If this is evident in your group, assure the members that you're concerned simply with the cultivation of inner quietness, which is fostering a value prominent in scripture. ("My soul waits in silence for God only" [Ps. 62:1]; "And Isaac went out to meditate in the field toward evening" [Gen. 24:63]; and so forth.) The same explanations may be necessary when presenting forms of prayer, reading, journaling, and other things the group may do. It is unfortunate that any of this needs to be explained. What a tragedy that we have forgotten our own spiritual roots and now attribute spirituality and its vocabulary exclusively to other faiths.

Though you personally may appreciate and use disciplines from other orientations, if this group is to be conducted in a church setting, assurance must be given that the organization's traditions will be congruent with the group's study and practice. A pastoral counseling center will need to assure potential group members that the theology of one particular group will not be promoted, and that many aspects of faith may be examined. As you can see, this first meeting is not only to assess the needs of the group, but also to establish the group's orientation as being trustworthy and safe. If someone remains doubtful about participating, be cordial, thank that person for her interest in coming, and *let her go.* Your purpose is not to whip up support for a spiritual growth group, but to carefully discover who may be ready for this step.

Agreeing on the Purpose

The convener and the members must be clear about the purposes of the group. If you are to be the convener of the first meeting, give some thought to the group's specific purpose as you envision it. (Before you read further, you may wish to note your own ideas, free from the influence of suggestions made below.) We discussed earlier, in chapter 1, the goals of this book in presenting spiritual formation as a group enterprise and objectives that are important for the group itself. Now, in the first meeting of the group, potential members need to gain a sense of the purpose of the group as it relates to them. How will what is done have an impact on them personally, and what will they learn? The purposes of the group might be as follows.

One purpose for the group is to learn something about the spiritual experiences of others, past and present. There are wonderful accounts written by Christian people of all cultures and in all ages, testifying to their encounters with the Holy. This is a legitimate part of our own history, and we are wise to learn about it. Reading and talking about these accounts, as well as hearing about the experiences of others in the group, greatly expands our ideas of what is possible for the human spirit.

Another important purpose is to foster the personal experience of God at a deeper level. As noted earlier, we cannot "order up" spiritual experience. We can, however, enter into an environment that is hospitable to the Holy. Although members will read or hear about the spiritual adventures of others, the goal is not that they say, "I must do this, too," or, "I just have to try harder and x-y-z will happen." The central task is to cultivate waiting—waiting on God. We are not in charge.

A third purpose is to accompany and support each other in our spiritual journeys. Spiritual growth can be lonely! When we wonder if what we are experiencing is normal, or when feelings are difficult to explain, we look around and usually decide not to make the effort to communicate. People do not commonly talk about their spiritual lives. It's like one's fears; they are often so closely guarded that nobody knows that anyone else has them. In this group the spiritual experience of each person should be acknowledged. The group is, above all, a hospitable place in which to share as we grow. Just as spiritual direction of the one-on-one style is a type of mentoring, so group members mentor one another in their spiritual quests.

It is important that the people attending this introductory meeting say what they hope for from this group experience. Later, as the group continues to meet, additional discussions may further refine and clarify the purposes of the group.

The Commitment

A very few beginning commitments should be required of members. The first is regular attendance, not a small commitment, as we all know. There are, of course, compelling reasons for not being in a particular meeting, ones anyone would understand. If a member simply cannot come, the convener should be notified so that the group can be conscious of the missing member and support that person with prayer.

This leads to the second commitment of group participants: that they pledge to pray for one another during the time between meetings. The effect on us of knowing that each day we are being remembered to God in the prayer of others is powerful.

The third agreement has to do with confidentiality. This will be addressed in a later chapter, but it is important to note here that what we hear from and know about the life of another is not the business of anyone outside the group. Anyone is free to speak for himself. But the ability to trust others in the group with one's story is critical to the growth of all. This must be made clear at the first meeting and occasionally repeated.

Time and Place

When there is general agreement as to the group's purpose and the commitment is clear, settle on a time and place and plan for the next meeting. Questions of time, place, and frequency of meetings are discussed in chapter 8. As for subsequent meetings, keep on reading and you will get some ideas about what is needed to begin well.

One question that will surely arise is whether this group is to be time limited, lasting several months to a year, or open-ended, going on as long as there is interest. You may not be able to make this determination at the first meeting. If there is uncertainty, consider a time limit with the option to continue. (Experience indicates that many groups continue in an open-ended format.)

Looking at a Typical Meeting

The remainder of this chapter gives an overview of a typical meeting. What will ninety minutes to two hours in a spiritual formation group be like? It is important to get a flavor of things before committing enthusiasm and energy. Following this overview of a typical meeting, chapters 4 through 7 will break down the four activities proposed for the group— prayer, study, sharing, and the creation of a personal daily pattern (a rule)—discussing each in greater detail.

I suggest meetings of an hour and a half or two hours. If you meet every week, the ninety minute format may work. Meeting longer and less often is a schedule that will suit some; many groups meet for two hours every week and thrive on the time together. What is presented here will assume a two-hour time frame. At the very beginning, I suggest meetings more often than once a month, to encourage familiarity and commitment. The members can determine what is best as they proceed. By the third or fourth meeting, members should know what works for them.

Quieting

After everyone is gathered, the first group task will be to quiet the inner chaos and distractions brought from our "exterior life." Spend just a few minutes in silence, with eyes closed, breathing slowly and deeply. After becoming more centered and focused, the convener can begin guiding the group through several areas of spiritual exploration. Gathering and quieting might take ten minutes.

Prayer, study, and sharing are the three things the group will do together. The fourth focus, "a rule," is carried out individually, outside the group. *Rule* is a word more familiar to Roman Catholics, so you may wish to substitute *daily pattern* for Protestant and evangelical groups. I use the word *rule* because of its long history and familiarity.

Prayer

Prayer is the group's starting activity, chosen because of its centering effect. Chapter 4 examines the different ways a person can pray, and there you can learn how this component can be presented. Most of us pray in only one, possibly two, ways. Experiencing new ways of communicating with God is exciting and will stretch you a bit. In the first meetings someone begins by briefly presenting one of the ways of praying, encouraging participants to try this style between meetings, and discussing their experiences at the next meeting.

Discussion of prayer and actually praying together might take twenty minutes. You may think that seems like much too short a time for something this important. It is. If the group decides to take longer, fine, but to do so you must cut time from study and sharing, which can be very wordy activities. Some will wish for unlimited time for prayer, study, and sharing. If that is chosen, you must consider the possibility of losing from the group those who are on a schedule and do not have the luxury of open-ended meeting time.

Study

The next forty minutes can be spent in study, which is not nearly enough time when people get interested. Chapter 5 will present suggested areas of study and some resources to be used. As the group progresses, members will develop new interests and no doubt propose fresh areas for future study.

The group should choose a particular area to study, with members presenting their contributions to the topic when their turn comes. Someone (or perhaps two people) will be responsible for presenting at each meeting. Distribute the assignments so that everyone can participate within the time frame allotted to the study. The member(s) presenting

the topic have the full forty minutes to relate their discoveries and allow
for questions and discussion. No one is expected to be an expert! Study
means just that: to inquire into something of interest. The presenter or
the group as a whole can decide how many sessions a particular study
will take. The convener is responsible for seeing that someone is pre-
pared to make a presentation, and that the agreed upon time schedule is
reasonably maintained.

Sharing

After a ten-minute break, perhaps with coffee or juice, the final forty
minutes of the two-hour time can be spent in sharing. Chapter 6 explores how this might work, giving suggestions for getting an exchange
started, and for seeing that everyone who wishes to talk gets a chance.

The importance of this component cannot be overestimated. The
shared, living experience of someone you know can be as rewarding and
instructive as any other activity in which the group engages. Learning
about the experiences of saints in the past is valuable, to be sure, but the
present-tense, week-to-week journey of a contemporary is priceless in
lighting one's own spiritual path.

At first some members will feel awkward and hesitant, feeling they
have little to say. Some may even decide not to join the group because
of a perceived expectation to participate in something that makes them
uncomfortable. During the first meeting, at which the group lays out the
purpose and format, make clear to participants that it is not necessary to
speak or share if they are not comfortable in doing so. Privacy is important, and the choice to listen and not contribute must be respected in
every member. This will be especially true for the prayer and sharing
times. It will be more important that every person take a turn in presenting a study, although there might be obvious exceptions. Keep in mind
that spiritual inquiry is new ground for many people. They may need
time to become familiar with the territory and with their feelings about
interior life. The very fact that they attend the group meetings says
something about their desire to grow. Generally, after only several
meetings, those who are now beginning to know one another at a significant personal level will begin to be "family," feeling the closeness and
rapport we all seek, but so seldom find in general society.

Ending and Benediction

The sharing conversation may be lively and excited or sometimes pen-
sive and sober. Either way, end the group session by again quieting,
eyes closed, breathing quietly, creating a sense of inner stillness. Members might bring to the group favorite prayers of benediction or, especially at first, the convener may choose one. It should be short, said in
unison, and give members a sense of what the Latin word *benediction*
means: a good word spoken. To put it another way, one should feel
blessed by hearing it. This quieting benediction time should take only a
few minutes, allowing you to end at the appointed time.

A Rule

This is not a group-session activity. It is a voluntary, daily activity that
some group members may do individually. It is a fascinating area for
study and is covered in chapter 7.

Early religious orders, such as the Benedictines and the Franciscans,
each had a "rule" characteristic of the order. These rules not only outlined the manner in which members conducted themselves, but also gave
members a daily framework within which they could stay focused on
God. There would be morning prayer, noon prayer, evening prayer, and
other prayer times in between. Some of the orders also had a time of
study, of work, and times of silence.

The current generation looks upon this kind of cloistered life as
either a luxury they wish they could afford or a restriction they believe
they could not bear to endure. We need not forfeit the benefits of such a
life just because it no longer fits with contemporary patterns. To be sure,
there are still cloistered orders practicing today, but their members are a
fractional part of the population. Those engaged in typical contemporary
life are the overwhelming majority. Surely there must be some way to
adapt to our own lives a workable daily framework for spiritual focusing.

We will explore ways to create a modern rule, one that is workable
for us in our own time. The Benedictine rule, a daily pattern of prayer,
study, and community begun in the seventeenth century, is a pattern still
compatible and adaptable to our own times; it is described in chapter 7.
A personal rule can include ways of serving others, whether individually

or as a group. Members should decide if they want to engage in the keeping of a rule; some will choose it, while others may not. You may well have as many versions of a rule as there are members in the group. The whole enterprise can get very interesting!

Summary

Whether your group is a random assortment or is clustered as to gender, age, zip code, or single/married status, the format should not stray too far from that outlined above. At the first meeting explain what the group will be about. You might present an outline of what the group will be doing in a typical meeting. Establish trust by saying that the activities will be in keeping with the faith perspective of the host organization, and that what is said and done will be confidential.

The group activities of praying, studying, and sharing are more fully described in the following chapters. A chapter about creating a modern rule is also included, should members choose to explore that. The group itself can decide when and where and how long to meet. The more welcome they feel to contribute to what is decided, the more ownership they will take in the group itself.

Whether you are a member of the clergy, a layperson, or someone associated with a counseling center, I hope there is less apprehension in your mind about starting a spiritual formation group in your church or counseling center. The benefits make the effort worthwhile.

CHAPTER 4

The Practice of Prayer

Prayer is the breath of the soul.
O. Hallesby

Prayer can be as natural as breathing. We forget that praying is not so much a wordy address as it is simply being in the presence of God. It may, indeed, be quite formal, as we experience in public places when someone rises to give verbal expression on behalf of the group. It can be as private as feeling the closeness of God during a walk in the woods. Some people pray by repeating a phrase. Others pray by stilling the mind and body. Still others like to pray with mental images or with the written word. So long as one is faced Godward and intends to connect with the Holy, prayer is taking place. As we pray, we make contact. We might just as well call it "exchange" or "interaction."

In the first few group sessions, it will be useful to spend the prayer segment discussing how all group members typically pray, if they do pray. What prayers of theirs have been particularly powerful or moving? Have they experienced moments of dryness or futility when prayer felt like a lead balloon that would not rise? Has anyone had an unusual prayer experience? It will be important for members not to try and compete to see who has had the greatest experience. All yearning toward God is legitimate prayer.

Most writers who discuss kinds of prayer list categories such as petition (asking), intercession, penitence, thanksgiving, and adoration. These delineations are useful, if somewhat rigid. The kinds of prayer I discuss in this chapter are not these categories. They are not about *what* we pray for, but *how* we go about it.

In this chapter I will most often refer to God as God, Creator, and the Holy. "The Holy," the name prominently used by Rudolf Otto, signifies the overwhelming mystery that is experienced as personal.[1]

Chapter 5 suggests topics that can be studied by the group. One of those topics is prayer and includes the study of two methods of praying developed in the past. What is covered here in chapter 4 can supplement that study.

Ways of Praying

Though there are many, many ways of praying, we will focus here on six that are easy to learn: formal prayer, conversational prayer, prayer using imagery, rhythmic prayer, journal prayer, and what is known as center- ing prayer. You may wonder why I suggest these several approaches; why not stick with what is most familiar? But familiar to whom? Many people pray in one or two of these ways without even thinking about it. What you see as familiar may be less so to another. It will be worth- while to explore a bit so as to broaden our experience.

Formal Prayer

Formal prayer is something to which we became accustomed as children and have heard throughout our lifetime. We think of formal prayer as a prayer that has a well-worked-out form and is used over time. I include in this definition any prayer that is said at a particular and expected time, even though it is extemporaneous and almost conversational. Meetings are often formally opened and closed with the audible saying of a prayer. You could say that "Now I lay me down to sleep" is a formal prayer taught to children. Some of the most beautiful formal prayers are found in church service liturgies. Their repetition is a source of great comfort and richness to those who use them over a lifetime, as attested to by prisoners of war and others in enforced solitude.

The great written prayers can prompt a spontaneous, "That is just what I want to say!" They express in beautiful or powerful language the feelings of our inmost beings and stretch out our spirits to embrace ever higher concepts. Consider the prayer of the Rozwi in South Africa.

Creator . . . who sews the heavens together like cloth,
Knit together everything here on the earth below.[2]

These eloquent sentences are taken from a formalized prayer that expresses the desire for harmony and wholeness in the world.

Notice how movingly and accurately Augustine talks of his search for God. Almost everyone shares some of the same feelings and wishes to say it half so well. We can be thankful that Augustine chose to record this prayer:

How late I came to love you, O beauty so ancient and so fresh, how late I came to love you! You were within me while I had gone outside to seek you. Unlovely myself, I rushed towards all those lovely things you had made. And always you were with me, and I was not with you. All these beauties kept me far from you—although they would not have existed at all unless they had their being in you. You called, you cried, you shattered my deafness. You sparkled, you blazed, you drove away my blindness. You shed your fragrance, and I drew in my breath, and I pant for you. I tasted and now I hunger and thirst. You touched me, and now I burn with longing for your peace. (401)[3]

For some simple lines that make a lovely family table grace, here is a verse from a poem by Georg Weissel, translated by Catherine Winkworth. The original, which is actually the third verse of the hymn "Lift Up Your Heads, Ye Mighty Gates," was written in first person. But if the "I" is changed to "we," these four lines are a nice alternative blessing at meals, as it asks us to focus more on inviting God to be with us than on asking God for plenty.

Redeemer, come, with us abide;
Our heart to thee we open wide;
Let us thy inner presence feel;
Thy grace and love in us reveal. Amen.

For a very contemporary prayer, these are the last lines of a supplication written by Robert Wood, from his book *A Thirty-Day Experiment in Prayer:*

Lord, reveal your presence to me everywhere, and help me
become aware of your presence each moment of the day.

May your presence fill the non answers, empty glances, and
lonely times of my life. Amen.[4]

The prayer books of several denominations are an obvious source
for classic formal prayers. *The Book of Common Prayer* is used by the
Anglican Communion (Episcopal Church in the U.S.). My favorite
prayer in this book is a "collect" for use on the fifth Sunday in Lent:

Almighty God, you alone can bring into order the unruly wills and
affections of sinners: Grant your people grace to love what you
command and desire what you promise; that, among the swift and
varied change of the world, our hearts may surely there be fixed
where true joys are to be found; through Jesus Christ our Lord, who
lives and reigns with you and the Holy Spirit, one God, now and for
ever. Amen.[5]

What better thing can we ask of God than that we have "grace to love
what you command and desire what you promise . . ."?

As you see, formal prayers are available from more sources than
one could ever hope to cover. These are but a few samplings and are
included to show how easily such prayers can become a part of our own
internal language. Not to read them and make them a part of our spiritual speech is to sentence ourselves to a certain kind of poverty.

During the spiritual formation group's twenty minutes set aside for
focusing on prayer, members might select several written prayers they
use or admire. Let each read them for the group in a prayerful manner,
giving plenty of time for the meaning to soak in. People may say why
this prayer was particularly meaningful to them. I suggest that each
person, at some time during this exposure to formal prayer, compose a
prayer and bring it to the next session. The composition can be traditional or more casual in language, long or short. It should express, as
well as one knows how, the deepest feeling of the author. Someone in
the group may offer to collect these prayers into a booklet for the
group's continuing use.

Conversational Prayer

Like formal prayer, conversational prayer is praying with words. Four
of the six forms of prayer presented here use words; we in the West are
most comfortable with that style. Indeed, it often does not occur to us
that one could pray without words.

Conversational prayer is like informal conversation with friends.
We simply start talking, saying what comes to mind. (As noted above,
some conversational prayer is offered publicly, but at a prescribed time.)
With friends, we make our words audible so they can know what we are
thinking. Because God hears the heart as well as the voice, we can communicate with words silently thought or verbally spoken. This implies
that we may cultivate what amounts to a running dialogue with the Spirit
of God within us. Frank Laubach, in his little classic, *Prayer*, talks about
flash prayers.[6] By this he means extremely brief prayers of ten seconds
to a minute. One might ask for guidance, give thanks, or pray for a situation that comes up. When my children were small and I was trying to
teach them how to pray in this way, I suggested they pray anytime they
heard a siren. Somebody, I told them, needs God's help right now. I
developed the habit myself, and now the joke is on me: I live on a cor-
ner between a fire station and the route to the hospital emergency room.

Praying in this sort of stream-of-consciousness manner assumes that
the pray-er is being heard, and that praying makes a difference in the
outcome of attitude or events. Very often the changed outcome occurs
in the person who prays, not in the external circumstance. The one who
prays may be newly sensitized to what is going on around her in a way
not noticed before. Another enormous benefit of this conversational
praying is the deepening sense that one is *accompanied* in life. Who
among us has not felt the despair of feeling utterly alone? Through conversational prayer, we gradually lose that feeling and come to know that
we are not isolated; someone walks alongside.

In conversational prayer our eyes are opened to the fact that God is
continually with us and also present in our surroundings. The poet
Gerard Manley Hopkins claimed that "The world is charged with the
grandeur of God." When one sees the world in this way, the question of
meaning in life becomes irrelevant because all life has meaning.

As the group experiments with conversational prayer, suggest that
participants try informally talking to God between meetings; ask them to

jot down some notes about how they responded to the experience. They may wish to comment on a particular incident—what they prayed about and the effect of the prayer. How did the total experience of extemporaneous prayer affect their sense of being with God? If group members are more accustomed to formal praying, how does it feel to have conversational prayer added to their repertoire? Ask those who have already used this style when they began to do so, and what it has meant for them during their lifetimes.

Prayer Using Imagery

Praying with words is familiar, but it is also possible to pray with mental pictures. Words, after all, are abstract symbols for some larger meaning we want to convey. Imagery is more primary and, like a picture, is worth a thousand words. Ann and Barry Ulanov have authored a fascinating book called *Primary Speech* in which they comment that "The language of primary-process thinking is not verbal. It comes in pictures and emotion-laden wishes and is private to ourselves, not really communicable, even though we share it.'"[7]

The word *image* is used here to mean a visualization we create with our minds. (In this instance it does not mean something we worship in the place of God.) Imagery is what we do when we try to imagine a scene or recall a place or person. We, in a sense, "see" it in our minds. "We can direct the mind's eye toward our inner world to bring about the creative forces of spirituality and healing in our daily life."[8]

Some people are more adept at seeing mental pictures than others, so if some group members do not respond well to this style of prayer, they should not feel bad. Participants should feel no differently about this than they would feel about not being as musical or artistic as someone else. (But I'll bet you can remember how many windows are in your living room. How did you do that?) Rachel Naomi Remen, M.D., a researcher in the field of imagery, believes that all people can image, but in different ways. She says some are visual, some auditory, and some kinesthetic.[9] We usually feel more comfortable with one or two styles of prayer than with the others. Word praying may be easiest for you and your group, but just try this method of imaging prayer and see how it goes. You may be surprised at the ease of using this mode.

While writing the above paragraph, I am interrupted by a telephone call from one of the clients I see for psychotherapy. She is distressed by what seems to her to be an insoluble dilemma. She wants to do one thing but is not able to let go of what must be forfeited if she is to move on in her decision. Each choice has equal weight for her, and she has been struggling with this problem for months. Two weeks ago she made what seemed a firm decision, but now she doubts that choice. She calls to say she is angry with herself for her indecision and exhausted with the entire effort. I clearly hear her distress.

Fortunately, this is a woman of deep faith. She is well acquainted with both formal and conversational types of prayer. At the moment, however, she is discouraged with words of any kind, and angry with herself and with God, who, she believes, has not told her what she should do. I suggest to her a visual image to pray with, a kind of praying she has never done before. "Imagine," I say, "that you are seated, and in your lap you see a large bowl. With your hands, place into the bowl all the distress and indecision you have carried with you now for so many months. Pick up the bowl, hold out your arms, and offer it all to God. Let go of it and say, 'Do with this whatever you like.' "

She tells me she has problems trusting right now and does not know if she can let go of the bowl. I suggest she tell God that she has difficulty trusting. She counters, "But what if I can't get the bowl back? This is scary!"

"You can take it back anytime you choose," I tell her, "along with the anxiety that goes with it."

"Okay!" she says. "I'll try it."

The purpose of this particular suggested imagery is to enable this person to stop the overcontrolling that keeps her frozen. She wants it all, as we all do, and has not been able to relinquish one good for the sake of a greater good. To use a New Testament image, she cannot sell her many pearls for the one pearl of great price. She insists on having all the pearls, which in this case is not possible. If she is able to relinquish the dilemma itself to God, and to *stay present and attentive to the situation*, she may be able to gain some insight and guidance about what she needs to do. As she said, "It's scary!" And it is. Placing our wants alongside God's purposes affects us. It is not that God high-handedly takes us over when we place our problems in God's care. Rather, it is *the way we see* our problems when we hold them alongside another perspective. Because of the contrast between our perception and what we believe to be

God's view, we are often able to see things clearly, at last. God answers us through our newfound perceptions.

I am very cautious about suggesting my own images for other people. I did so with this person because she needed concrete direction, and in our telephone conversation we were time limited. The convener and other group members should resist the temptation to quickly supply images for others. It works much better if the one praying creates his own images. Before you decide to use this way of praying, decide what it is you are seeking to have or to know. If it is to control a person or a situation, I suggest you rethink the whole enterprise. If what you want is, as the collect (prayer) puts it, "grace to love what you [God] command and desire what you promise," then you are likely to get the thing for which you ask. *Prayer is not for coercing a result. It is for "union with."*

Here is a way to practice prayer using imagery. Place yourself within a prayerful mental framework by closing your eyes and imagining a picture of great peacefulness and safety. It can be a mountain meadow, a strand of seashore, or, as one of my clients related, "my grandmother's front porch." It will be your place alone, and you may return to it at any future time. Imagine the temperature, the season of the year, the background sounds, and the whole feel of the place. Now put yourself into the scene and become aware of the presence of the Holy in this environment. Perhaps you will conjure a table before you or a rock or just bright sunlight. Perhaps none of these things will be what you see. Whatever you image, this must be a sacred and safe place for you. Create the scene in which you feel you belong. As the Ulanovs say, "The language of primary-process thinking is not verbal."[10] In this instance, your pictures are your prayer.

As you imagine this scene, say whatever you wish, do whatever you wish, or simply *be* without saying or doing anything. Perhaps you need to rest without the slightest activity. This sort of rest is not drowsiness, as your mind will be very attentive and alert. You may, like my client, want to place your troubles in a bowl or a basket and offer them to God, waiting attentively as you do so. Place the bowl on the table, rock, or whatever "altar" you imagine.

"How long should I do this?" An entirely logical question for logical people who faithfully follow instruction booklets. Do this as long as it takes. Participants may feel comfortable in their imagery for a couple of minutes or may decide to stay for twenty minutes or more. If some in the group decide to extend the time, they should simply stay in a very receptive mood. No one needs to feel in the least responsible for creating the next thing. You will find that images come to you all on their own, without help. People as goal oriented as we in the West have difficulty waiting peacefully with a listening attitude. We want so much to achieve something. This kind of praying is not about achieving. Once we are in our imagined setting, we have already arrived where we need to be.

The biblical record shows us some expert practitioners of imagery. Isaiah comes to mind, with his description of the six-winged angels and of the hot coal in his mouth. The images conveyed by John in Revelation are powerful and vivid. One's own images may not always be as dramatic as theirs, and we may or may not choose to record them in words at a later time, but the mental pictures are extremely important in that they arise in us while we are in God's presence. Do not belittle your own experience!

When group members decide to try this method of praying, they may first want to sit quietly, doing it together. The convener can read aloud the above paragraph about picturing a place of great peacefulness and safety. After about ten minutes, the convener can ask participants to share their images and the effect of the experience. I predict that this will be one of the group's most easily discussed topics. The shared experience of each will answer the questions of others. People will then feel more secure trying this on their own.

Although I have met only one person with a personal objection to praying with images, we should anticipate this possibility. Anyone uncomfortable with this way of praying should stop without hesitation. The person may have very good reason for this choice, and it is, after all, not an achievement or a competition. It is an option.

There are several other ways of praying using visualization, particularly with images from scripture. Two of these will be discussed in chapter 5, under the subheading Prayer.

Rhythmic Prayer

We are a busy people. The idea of retreating to a cloister to cultivate our connectedness to God seems like a luxury that is beyond practical consideration. Let's not despair. I believe we have wrung our collective hands over our modern busyness much too long. It is time to stop complaining and to start being creative in shaping a more contemporary pattern for daily spirituality, one that meshes with our reality. One approach is learning to pray in ways that fit with our common life. We are wise, of course, to take some time apart and be reflective at the beginning and the close of the day, though I admit that it is difficult to carve out that island, especially amid a growing family. Because of our pressures, we need a way to pray-on-the-run.

Group members who are walkers or runners will easily grasp this "rhythmic" way of praying. They will know how it is to clip along at a nice even pace and hear a fragment of a tune running over and over in their heads to the beat of their stride. There is something soothing and satisfying about walking to a musical phrase. Try, instead, substituting a prayer phrase repeated again and again to the rhythm of your steps. The phrase might come from the Book of Psalms, from the gospels, from a hymn sung last Sunday, or it might be a brief statement or word that inspires you. Here are examples from these very sources. Can you imagine walking along to these cadences?

"The Lord is my shepherd, I shall not want" (Ps. 23:1).

"Lord, if you will, you can make me clean" (Luke 5:12).

"Amazing grace, how sweet the sound . . . . I once was lost, but now am found."

All life is a gift.

Lov-ing-kind-ness.

In medieval monasteries, and occasionally in modern ones, you will see what is called a "close," which is an open area enclosed by buildings. Around the perimeter some enclosures have porches along which one

can walk in shelter from one building to the another. Monks often
walked the porches expressly as a physical exercise as they were spiritually exercising—repeating some scripture or prayer. What a peaceful
and focused way to move!

We also walk. Too often we tend to think of walking in terms of
stress—hurrying to a meeting or getting to work—or in terms of pushing
for athletic achievement. Why not, like the monks, think of it as prayer?

Not every walk or jog needs to be thought of in this way; that could
become obsessive. But from time to time, when we have the desire to
quiet ourselves or to lift our spirits to God, we can choose a phrase and
walk, joining our minds and spirits and bodies in this rhythmic synthesis.
Of course a person in a wheelchair or immobilized in some way is equally able to engage in rhythmic prayer. A phrase can be paced to the natural rhythm of one's breath. This is a creative way to allow the agitation
of confinement to be soothed.

There is precedent in both Christian and Jewish traditions for this
sort of praying. The Christian classic in this field is *The Way of a Pilgrim* written in about 1869 by a Russian *starets* or holy man.[11] The book
tells of a man who prayed his way across Russia reciting a single phrase.
My favorite phrase for rhythmic prayer is Hebrew and comes from the
Jewish mantra meditation most often suggested for this mode of prayer.
The phrase is *Ribbono shel Olam*, meaning Master of the Universe; it
was used as early as the first century B.C.E. by Simeon ben Shetach,
and according to the Talmud, was used in New Testament times.[12] The
phrase prayerfully puts me in tune with the oneness of God and the
wholeness of creation. Try saying it in sequences of three steps or beats,
one for each word. If you're walking, the uneven number will make you
begin the phrase on alternate feet. If you find that distracting, choose
some phrase with an even number of syllables.

Journal Prayer

Written journal prayers are not the same as printed "formal" prayers.
Journal prayers might well be called letters to God. I realized the power
of this sort of writing when I began suggesting it to clients who had difficulty coming to terms with the truth about their lives. We often say that
people don't really want to know the truth about some things, that they

deliberately suppress and repress the dark side of themselves. Well, yes and no. The issue is not that we don't want to know the truth; it is that we fear that the truth will destroy us. We do not trust that the truth will actually set us free. I believe that, deep down, we do want to understand ourselves. Why else would people brave therapy?

Writing letters to God is a way of accessing the truth in safe company! Have you ever been amazed at how you can stew around about something troublesome, unable to break through the confusion, and then see it all clearly as you begin to bring it into God's presence? Bringing our thoughts into the atmosphere of prayer enhances perspective. Writing it out is even more powerful than thinking it or saying it. In writing we engage both mind and body, and writing slows us enough to actually work out our thoughts and feelings. I recommend writing in longhand using cursive style. This method engages the right side of the brain, the more creative part, and helps us to focus in a meditative way.

When it is time to begin journal prayer, each member in the group will want to get a book with blank pages. This will help participants be intentional about their commitment to pray in a journal. The kind of blank book is immaterial, as long as it suits the owner. I have seen everything from Big Chief tablets to leather bound books embossed with the owner's initials.

Several times a week, each member of the group can commit to write a letter to God or, if preferred, a comment to God on paper. The writing can be chatty and casual, formal and poetic. If God speaks all languages, then God can certainly respond to one's personal style. The length of what one writes depends on how one best expresses oneself. Some people find writing their prayer so therapeutic that they fill pages and pages, finding that the writing itself is clarifying. Others express themselves best in a brief but well-worked sentence or two. Occasionally one might come to the page and write something like, "Sorry, but I have nothing to say right now."

There's value in having a book full of pages, instead of writing these prayers on random scraps of paper; over a period of time, we as writers can trace the trajectory of our development in the matters that become the subject of prayer. We are able to observe our growth in learning to trust God with complaints as well as enthusiasms. Occasionally we laugh at the fact that what we wanted "more than anything" two months ago now matters so little to us. Noticing these things may be something some members eventually choose to share with the group.

Remember that journal prayer is, above all, private prayer. If group members want to share some of it with others, that may be helpful for them and perhaps for the group. If they do not, they should not! The worst possible thing to happen in journal prayer is for the writer to unconsciously "edit" for some unseen reader. A word of caution: If you start thinking about how what you have just written will be heard by the group, decide at once that you will not read to others any of what you've written. The hearer, remember, is God. How often do you suppose that public prayer is crafted for the assembled hearers and not addressed to God? We know it happens all the time. This misdirection is not the intent of a private prayer journal.

Speaking of privacy, keep your journal in a private space. Leaving it out for others to pick up and read is setting them up for your anger. If there is something in the journal you hope they will "accidentally" find, stop. Remember, again, you are writing to God. And you might write to God about how you need the courage and tact to say out loud what you want someone to know.

If you are one of those people for whom English was the most dreaded of classes or someone who avoids personal letter writing, do not despair. I strongly suspect that God is not a literary critic, but one who values honesty far above length and style. As the Ulanovs say, "The desire for prayer is the desire for a meeting with truth."[13]

Centering Prayer

"Skepticism is the chastity of intellect," said George Santayana. And group members may be most skeptical about meditative prayer. I urge your group to persevere and consider this prayer type. Some members may decide this is not for them, but each person should know what it is about and appreciate those who use it. This is a meditative prayer that can lead to profound experiences of peace, insight, and even the transcendent. As with all things worthwhile, meditative prayer requires some discipline.

There are numerous methods and approaches for praying meditatively. All of the approaches are characterized by an inner stillness and attentive waiting on God. One can rest in this meditative kind of prayerfulness for a few minutes or for an hour or more. Because of its simplicity, I have chosen an approach that is currently called centering prayer.

Two popular proponents of this approach are Basil Pennington and Thomas Keating. Pennington's book is titled *Centering Prayer*.[14] Keating also has a book explaining this prayer style called *Intimacy with God*,[15] as well as a series of videotapes in which he effectively presents his ideas in a teaching format.[16] The books, especially Keating's, are good teachers of the method, and the tapes are just extra help. I would warn the convener that nothing will so quickly kill a spiritual growth group as anticipating that the time set aside for prayer will be spent in watching a series of five, hour-long tapes. If tapes are used, let one member review them and present what she has learned to the others. Tapes can be circulated to group members who want to view them outside the meeting time.

For the sake of brevity, here is the very short set of guidelines given by Keating. Keep in mind that Pennington and Keating have written entire books about centering prayer, and that reading just these few directions will not be all the group needs to become proficient. These guidelines do, however, demonstrate how simple the method is and give a sense of what centering prayer is about. It is at least enough to begin.

1. Choose a sacred word as the symbol of your intention to consent to God's presence and action within [explained below].

2. Sitting comfortably and with eyes closed, settle briefly and silently introduce the sacred word as the symbol of your consent to God's presence and action within.

3. When you become aware of thoughts, return ever-so-gently to the sacred word. [Keating is suggesting turning away from thoughts that distract one from focusing on the sacred word.]

4. At the end of the prayer period, remain in silence with eyes closed for a couple of minutes.[17]

Don't let the term "sacred word" put anyone off. This word just expresses the intention to be open to God, and there is nothing at all magic about its selection. Words suggested by Keating are *God*, *Abba*, and *peace*. The Hebrew word *ruach*, pronounced *roo*-ahkh, refers to both wind and spirit. Used in the creation story (Gen. 1:2), it means "the wind from God." Practitioners of meditative prayer may find it especially satisfying to use this word as they notice their breathing and focus on the idea of *spirit as breath*.

This reference to breath brings up an important point. Centering prayer requires a quiet spirit and a relaxed body. People coming into the group after a long day of work and a traffic-hour drive will be tense and anxious. Ask them to notice where their breath is going, probably high up in the chest and just below the collar bone. This is where we breathe when we are stressed. Ask participants to place their right hands on their upper chests and their left hands at their waists, left thumbs at their belt buckles. Now ask them to breathe down to their left hands, filling the lower part of the lungs first, so that the abdomen lifts up and down slowly with each breath. (If the right hand is rising and falling, breathing is not deep enough.) Within a few seconds they will discover their bodies beginning to relax and their minds focusing on the present moment rather than on the stresses of the day.

At this time much is being written about techniques of breathing, and some individual in the group may want to take a side excursion, investigating this on his own. A good general book is one by psychologist Gay Hendricks, who specializes in whole body therapy.[18] One treatment that specifically connects breathing and prayer is *The Breath of God* by Nancy Roth.[19] Another that deals with breath and prayer is *The Breath of Life* by Ron DelBene.[20] As far as we are concerned here, breathing technique is not the group's primary focus; quieting the mind and body so that we can pray is the intent. Breathing naturally and in a relaxed way is just one way to help with that intent.

"What shall I think about?" This question can provoke anxiety and even anger in some who try centering prayer. It is difficult for us to think of this quiet praying as being anything but a project that we must control or direct. The whole point is that *when one listens to another, the "other" is in charge.* Your only task is to be open and quiet and attentive. That is all you do. "But what will I hear? This is spooky." No, it is just unfamiliar. Have you never been with someone with whom you were so close that you were able for a while to sit with that person wordlessly, yet comfortably? God is even better able than that person to communicate to us through feelings, impressions, peacefulness, questions—all sorts of things. "Silence is the language God speaks, and everything else is a bad translation," says Keating.[21]

When we practice a meditative, receptive type of prayer, we are often bothered by the fact that our minds flit about endlessly in random, broken thoughts. Aggravated because of our inability to stay centered, we scold ourselves and say we "can't do it." That is the reason for using what Keating calls the sacred word. Without in the least becoming impatient with yourself, gently return to the word, as you would to an oasis, and take up the centering peacefulness again. In the beginning, you will be able to sustain your center only momentarily and occasionally. As you continue, you will begin to enjoy longer periods of returning to this spiritual oasis. Gregory the Great, in the sixth century, called this contemplative tradition a "resting in God." Centering prayer is so simple and easy that it is, oddly enough, difficult, and so requires time and discipline. If you become able to use this way of praying, you may find it to be the tranquil island in your day, indeed, the centering anchor for your life.

To begin, ask group members to engage in centering prayer together for about ten minutes or more. Afterward, ask them what sacred word they chose and what its meaning is for them. Suggest that centering prayer be done by each at least once a day during the time between the group's meetings. Following each time of private centering prayer, members might jot down just a sentence or two about their impression of the experience. This will refresh their minds and make more concrete an experience that is somewhat amorphous. Journaling after this kind of prayer is extremely valuable. Often we understand that something has happened only after we write it down. Keep in mind that what you are doing is relationship, not achievement. The wisdom of Oswald Chambers helps us here: "God is not working toward a particular finish: His end is the process. . . . What men call training and preparation, God calls the end."[22]

Is Prayer Worth the Effort?

This is a legitimate question and we should have no patience with those who will not allow it to be asked. Victor Frankl observes that "What is to give light must endure burning."[23] Prayer takes, at the very least, our time, quite a bit of energy, and certainly our mental and physical focus. We are right to ask why we should do it. For many it is enough that Jesus instructs us to pray. Actually, if one is a follower of Jesus, that is sufficient reason. But wouldn't you like to know, all things considered, if it makes a difference?

We usually feel that prayer is worth the effort if the outcome of prayer is what we want. Much prayer is offered regarding the healing of diseases and the prevention of accidents. Many can testify that prayer indeed was the healing force and the preventer of calamity in their lives or in the life of one they know. But what about equally worthwhile people who prayed just as sincerely and fervently and saw disease or accident take the life of one for whom they prayed? Did they not "do it right," or is God to blame? Anxiously and obsessively praying for specific outcomes is what I call *controlling prayer*. It can be an attempt to persuade or influence to the ends we have determined "best." It is more than understandable that we feel compelled to pray for certain things to happen. We are, after all, anxious about ourselves and those we love, all of us negotiating every day in a capricious world. We desperately fear loss.

In their discussion of prayer, the group will be helped by the insights of others who have struggled with how and when to pray. Paul's instruction to the Thessalonians was to "pray without ceasing," and in Luke 18 Jesus admonishes the hearer to pray continually. Perhaps this is best understood as what another tradition calls "mindfulness." "Prayer," says Larry Dossy, "tends to follow instructions laid down by the great religious traditions; prayerfulness does not. It is a feeling of unity with the All."[24] The Lord's Prayer, which Christians consider the ultimate model for the way one should pray, presents "thy will be done" to be the highest and most appropriate request. The gospels report that Jesus prayed this way in Gethsemane before his crucifixion. It is as if the composer of the model prayer recognizes that disease, accident, and death are natural life events; that some are spared and some are not. We are encouraged to ask the Creator for what we desire, as did Jesus, and then, above all, for what is best in a given instance. It may be that our walking *through* the event with God is the "best."

Glenn Hinson writes about what we can expect in prayer, and about the God who doesn't "come through."[25] Most of us grew up hearing that "prayer changes things." If we do not see the change for which we hope, we tend to think that prayer is not worth the effort. If what we seek, however, is inner change, either in ourselves or in others, we may indeed see prayer as having worth. Does this imply that our prayer for specific

things is not effective or that we should not pray for particular outcomes? No. We continue to pray for what we hope. We are, after all,
told by Jesus in a Luke 18 prayer parable to be persistent, asking again
and again. What we do want to remember is that prayer is not a drug, a
vitamin, or a hex. Rather, it is our cooperation with God in the world.
Instead of becoming fixated on outcomes, we are to lean more toward
intentions: God's and ours. There are times when our inner change is
more needed than any outward change. Rather than attend to this inner
maturity, we choose to believe fulfillment comes from the achievement
of health, wealth, and unending youth. As Susan Ertz has put it, "Mil-
lions long for immortality who do not know what to do with themselves
on a rainy Sunday afternoon."[26]

Defining for ourselves what prayer is and why it is worth our energy
becomes a primary inquiry for the person of spirit. I like the statement
of a priest quoted by Caroline Myss: "Authentic prayer does not mean to
turn to God in order to get something; it means to turn to God in order to
be with someone." That beautifully explains the purpose of praying! He
further defines prayer for himself by saying, "Prayer is not so much our
words to God as our life with God."[27]

Engagement in various kinds of praying is, in itself, not of great importance. What is important for the group's members is experiencing the
best paths for opening to God's presence so that, consciously or unconsciously, every moment of life can be spent in this extraordinary companionship. That, at least to me, seems like having so much more than
just changed circumstances.

CHAPTER FIVE

"Read, Mark, and Inwardly Digest"

Blessed Lord, who caused all holy Scriptures to be written for our learning: Grant us so to hear them, read, mark, learn, and inwardly digest them, that we may embrace and ever hold fast the blessed hope of everlasting life, which you have given us in our Savior Jesus Christ; who lives and reigns with you and the Holy Spirit, one God, for ever and ever. Amen.

The Book of Common Prayer

This prayer of Thomas Cranmer, composed in 1549 and based on Romans 15:4, is good advice for what we are now setting out to do: to hear, read, mark, learn, and inwardly digest. The prayer refers to the reading of scripture and some groups will want to confine their studies to the Bible. In groups for which knowledge of scripture is minimal, this focus may be a good choice. In the discussion in this chapter, we will be looking at many sources, and a biblical connection can be made with each topic. The medieval monastics called the study part of their discipline *spiritual reading*. We will use the word *study*, but it is study of a particular kind. As we study, we learn to listen to the voice of God and others who tell of God. The goal of the group's study is to widen and enrich: widen their understanding of what spiritual experiences have been possible for others, and enrich their experience of the pervasive and interactive influence of God in the lives of people. We can only do what we can first imagine, and learning about the spiritual journeys of others helps us to imagine something wider than our own experience. We may or may not choose to walk the path another walks, but our understanding of the scope of God's interaction with people makes possible needed perspective.

The amount of time suggested for this study component is about forty to forty-five minutes. Although the group may agree to read the same material simultaneously, there is some merit in letting members take different readings within the same subject. In the following study titled Spiritual Development, for instance, the group can look over available material, then each person can choose a reading assignment of particular interest. One may choose to work with personality types, another with Fowler's explanation of stages of faith, and another with one of the other resources suggested. More than one person can read the same material, of course, but the wider the breadth of what is read, the greater the variety and contribution during the discussion time. A time limit for the subject can be agreed on (maybe four or five meetings per topic). The group may want to allow some flexibility, should a topic prove to be more interesting or less interesting than anticipated.

Ask each member to present to the group what he or she has studied, taking responsibility ahead of time for a particular date. Two people might decide to present together. It is best if the presentation is informal, encouraging questions and comments as the presenter talks about the material. Think of this as a group effort, not as a formal paper on which one is graded by peers. Favorite or puzzling passages can be read, background given, and opinion expressed as to the value of an author's thought.

Should you discover that the book you want to read for your study is out of print, become a detective. Your local book shop may be able to direct you to secondhand bookstores that specialize in religious books. Look in the *Yellow Pages* of the largest city near you. Stores will usually take credit-card telephone orders and mail books. See the endnotes for names of several secondhand bookstores that specialize in religious books or have a department that does.[1] For an array of books that are currently in print, refer to the endnotes of chapter 7, where you will find some suggestions of catalogs featuring religious books.

Another avenue, should you not find a specific book suggested here, is to select a book on the same subject. (The works of many of the acknowledged, classic writers introduced here are analyzed, discussed, or condensed by more contemporary writers.) The study suggestions in this chapter recommend several books that can be read in each area. And again, the group might choose to study together only one book. This is the typical format of many study groups. Whichever format you use, be sure to limit your study selection to those books that clearly address the spiritual life—or spirituality. If you have no idea where to start, I suggest a wonderfully entertaining book by C. S. Lewis, *The Screwtape Letters*.[2] It is short, readable, discussable, and available in many editions. Everyone will identify with Lewis's witty yet profound treatment of sin and virtue.

As your group progresses, consider these additional areas of study, to read, mark, learn, and inwardly digest.

A Reading Sampler

This is a broad category of study and can be taken up at different times by the group. What follows is a taste of different types of books and a sampling from different centuries. The real treasure is in discovering and gaining knowledge in some particular strand of writing that fascinates the reader. These suggestions just skim the surface, but from here you may venture into the woods that, as Frost says, are lovely, dark, and deep—and are full of the riches that are our Christian legacy.

Some "Get Acquainted" Collections

This makes a good place to begin. These sampler suggestions involve dipping your toe in the waters of spiritual writings. Suggested books are edited collections of short selected writings. The nice thing about this particular study is that it can continue for a few weeks, stop to make way for other topics, and then be taken up again at a later time. It can also serve as a refreshing break after engaging in a rather heavy study. I would suggest that the group not spend weeks and weeks sampling readings. It might be useful to read in the "collections" books for awhile, then move on to a more concentrated study, several of which are outlined later in this chapter.

There are so many fine collections of quotations from spiritual writers that one hardly knows how to select only a few. You will have your own favorites, which you may have used and want to share with the group. One of the very best samplers of spiritual writings is *A Guide to Prayer for Ministers and Other Servants*, edited by Rueben Job and

Norman Shawchuck.[3] Don't be put off by the title. This is not a book
for clergy only. I don't believe the editors had any idea how wide a
readership the book would enjoy, or they would have named it *A Guide
to Prayer and Readings for Absolutely Everybody*. This book of daily
readings and a sequel, *A Guide to Prayer for All God's People*, essentially skim the cream from some of the best spiritual writers.[4] The range
crosses denominational boundaries and spans several centuries from
Saint Augustine to William Barclay, from C. S. Lewis to Carlo Caretto,
and Teresa of Avila to Mother Teresa of Calcutta.

In a sampler like this members of the group can find writers to
whom they deeply respond. Encourage them to look for that person who
speaks to their present needs or whose writing resonates with their own
spirituality. They can look for the book or books from which that writer's quotations are taken and track down other books by that author.
You may have found "your person," at least for this point in your life.
Books by or about this person will often include a biography. Get to
know the author and allow him or her to be among your mentors, one
who enriches your own spiritual formation.

Though difficult to locate, another fine sampling of spiritual writing
is *The Lord of the Journey*, a collection focusing on the Reformed,
evangelical tradition of spirituality.[5] Those who think that writings in
spirituality are housed only within earlier traditions can read this and
rejoice. Another Reformed collection of quotations is *Minister's Prayer
Book*, a collection originally intended for Lutheran clergy, but enjoyed
by people in all denominations.[6] Although not arranged specifically as
daily readings, these two books have short entries and can be used in that
way.

I recommend two easily found books that are samplers presented as
daily readings, one a classic and another that may become so. You will
not go wrong in considering the little volume by Oswald Chambers, *My
Utmost for His Highest*.[7] It has been an inspirational mainstay for sixty
years, and its wise ideas are timeless. Another very good book is *Listening to Your Life*, a collection of daily meditations taken from the more
than twenty books by Frederick Buechner.[8] Many see Buechner as the
best of the current religious writers. Unlike the previously cited books,
which sample the work of many writers, the Chambers and Buechner
books contain rich excerpts from the writings of one person, giving you
the opportunity to know the author's mind and extraordinary spirit.

A friend of mine who is a working mother of toddlers says that as much as she wishes to read long and deeply, the page-a-day sort of book is all she can manage for now. The books suggested above are especially good for any whose lives are under severe time constraints.

Writings from the Mystics

In this section I had originally intended to suggest basic readings, fundamental to an informed history of Christian spirituality. The list is so vast, even when pared down, that I admittedly suggest only a very few, acknowledging that many readers will be horrified at what I have omitted.

To begin, see if you can get a copy of Urban T. Holmes's little paperback, *A History of Christian Spirituality.*[9] To my knowledge it remains out of print. You may be able to borrow it from an Episcopal clergyperson, as it was popular in those circles, or try contacting a secondhand book source or The Anglican Bibliopole.[10] Knowing it is out of print, I would not suggest it except that it provides excellent, very short reviews of the Christian mystic writers, including titles of their major works. There are other fine books that contain some of this information, and you may come across one. But none is so comprehensive or well organized as Holmes. You will not need such a book to engage in this study; it simply provides a good overview of the mystic writers for the serious student.

As to the basics, it will be important to get a flavor of the work of Saint Augustine, especially the *Confessions.* This may seem daunting to the first-time reader of Augustine, so I suggest *An Augustine Reader,* or any such overview, which gives representative selections of his thought.

An interesting portrait of seven women mystics is offered in Carol Lee Flinders's *Enduring Grace.*[12] (For those into vegetarian cooking, she is the author of the popular *Laurel's Kitchen* cookbooks.) Flinders profiles Clare of Assisi, Mechthild of Magdeburg, Julian of Norwich, Catherine of Siena, Catherine of Genoa, Teresa of Avila, and Thérése of Lisieux. I assure you, all of them are interesting. Especially fascinating is the picture of life in centuries past for women who felt compelled to live out a spiritual calling. Flinders provides a very good list of books about each woman. You traverse many trails here as you read not only about these women, but also their actual writings. Julian of Norwich and Teresa of Avila are two about whom you must know. Just so you can talk about it out loud, Norwich is pronounced *Nor*-itch.

During the Middle Ages, two important men writing about the spiritual life were Francis of Assisi and Meister Eckhart. The reader will find many books, both scholarly and beautiful, adult and juvenile, with text by Saint Francis. You may especially enjoy starting with a biography about his remarkable life. He is, by the way, the author of that well-loved prayer "Lord, make me an instrument of thy peace." One delightful book is *The Flowers of St. Francis of Assisi.*[13] Browse a bit and you will discover that Saint Francis deserves to be more than just a piece of benevolent garden concrete! The German Meister Eckhart is one of those thinkers who belongs in our own age as much as in his own. There are several good translations of his work including the popular *Breakthrough: Meister Eckhart's Creation Spirituality in New Translation* by Matthew Fox.[14] Eckhart, representative of a group called the Rhineland mystics, is well worth the time it will take you to delve into his thought. Have a pencil ready to underline; he is very quotable.

Two classics offered by several publishers are *The Imitation of Christ* by Thomas a Kempis and *The Practice of the Presence of God* by Brother Lawrence. The latter is charming in its simplicity and a bit more palatable to modern tastes and thought, but both are musts on the bookshelf of the serious reader in spirituality. Another more recent and essential classic is the *Journal* by John Woolman, an eighteenth-century American Quaker.[15] With Woolman, as with all writing of earlier eras, the reader should take into account "the times" and the spirituality prevalent within that culture. Some ideas do not easily adapt to contemporary frameworks, but we will be poorer without these priceless insights from past practitioners of the spiritual life.

Favorite Contemporary Writers

Nobody liked to write about spirituality as much as Evelyn Underhill. This British theologian, who wrote in the early part of the twentieth century, is both informational about the history of spirituality and inspirational. She is so inspirational that she sometimes asks for more than we may feel we can give. See for yourself. You might start with her small book called *The Spiritual Life*, then move on to *Mysticism*, a study of the nature and history of human spiritual consciousness.[16] This second book will introduce you to many other names important in the field of spirituality.

A Testament of Devotion is a wonderful little book of essays by Quaker Thomas Kelly, assembled in 1941 following his death.[17] It is mystical in a quite different sense from Underhill, exhibiting the Quaker qualities of being direct, grounded, and uncomplicated.

The literary person who favors poetry and poetic writing will enjoy the modern classic *Markings* by Dag Hammarskjold, secretary-general of the United Nations from 1953 to 1961.[18] Hammarskjold left the manu-script behind to be published after his death, which occurred in 1961 as the result of an air crash. This intimate diary, not unlike Pascal's *Pensées*, is written in short fragments and makes for fine meditative reading.

Three late twentieth-century writers who have captured the minds of those looking for "something more" are Thomas Merton, Henri Nouwen, and Richard Foster. Each published many titles, all of them worth looking into. If you are just starting out with Merton, read his *No Man Is an Island*, which presents his best thoughts in a bit-by-bit format that makes for good stop-and-start reading.[19] A good introduction to Henri Nouwen is *The Genesee Diary*.[20] This early work, published in 1976, presents his insights on the spiritual life as it gives the reader a glimpse of Nouwen negotiating his own spiritual journey while visiting a Trappist monastery. Also important to this list of contemporary writers is Richard Foster, whose book *Celebration of Discipline* was the first of several celebrating Christian life.[21] This Quaker writer is steeped in the classics of spirituality yet entirely original in his own work.

It is overwhelming to consider the endless treasure found in spiritual writing. Again, I apologize to the reader who is aghast that his favorites have not been mentioned. But as we have said before, start on the trail and it will lead you down more and more varied terrain. Ask people whose spiritual life you admire to tell you what author or thought has been most influential in their development. That will lead you to more diversity, and into some new avenues of spiritual reading.

Spiritual Development

This discussion of study resources delves into a more clinical approach
to spiritual development, considering how it is that people grow and
develop. Here we consider spirituality through the lens of the discipline
of psychology. People may be put off by this idea at first. How, we ask,
can spirituality be put under a microscope or be quantified? It is true
that interior life is so subjective that only good guesses can be made
about its norms. Nonetheless, it always proves interesting, even helpful,
when we delve into the "why" of a thing. In presenting this kind of
material, my experience indicates that it is one of the most engaging and
spiritually growth-producing studies of all. After all, what is more interesting to us than ourselves?

Here are several books and some testing instruments that are valuable in showing how to understand each group member's unique spirituality. Keep in mind that this is not an effort to determine good/bad, or
good, better, best. Rather, it is a help to self-understanding. It is somewhat like saying that some people are blondes and some brunettes.
Neither is "better," but there is a difference that makes for variety and
value. Understanding the differences and the contributions each makes
is important in identifying the strengths of each group member and
opens up new areas of growth and appreciation.

The favorite of this genre is the Myers Briggs Temperament Indicator (MBTI). People interested in a spiritual formation group may well
have taken this test in the past. If anyone has not taken the MBTI within
the last six months, ask her to do so again. It is a good thing for everyone in the group to have access to the paperback *Please Understand Me,*
which has a shortened version of the indicator test in the back.[22] The
results are of no value without the book's explanations. As companions
to *Please Understand Me*, also read *Prayer and Temperament* by
Michael and Norrisey,[23] and *Gifts Differing* by Isabel Briggs Myers.[24] I
suggest these two additional books because they focus on applying the
MBTI insights to spiritual experience, which is, after all, what the group
is about.

During the sessions devoted to this typology, consider discussion
that explores how what is learned about type affects one's spiritual life
and expression. How is it that my temperament influences the way in
which I approach and interact with God? The group may want to spend

several sessions on this intriguing subject. At minimum, members would become well enough acquainted with the material so that those who have an interest in going further into the subject can do so on their own.

A ground-breaking book in the field of religious development has been *Stages of Faith* by James Fowler.[25] Fowler describes the stages of development through which a person may pass as he or she matures in faith. Since this 1981 publication, Fowler's research has been built upon and taken further by him and by others. He has been faulted, as have other developmental psychologists, for not taking into account the different maturational processes of women, an issue addressed by Carol Gilligan in her equally important work, *In a Different Voice*.[26] Gilligan explains that women's moral development is framed on the basis of relationships, while that of men is framed in terms of rules. She points out that both are needed, but both must first be understood. This pair of books can make a very insightful study and can foster an enlightening male-female dialogue. Both authors are writing for professionals in their field, and, though both are "readable," you will have to exercise a little patience. It doesn't matter if you understand every phrase, word, and concept. Go for the bottom line of what these two outstanding thinkers are saying.

If developmental study becomes important for members, I recommend these additional titles: *The Evolving Person* by Robert Kegan,[27] chapter 7 of Scott Peck's book *Further along the Road Less Traveled,*[28] *New Passages* by Gail Sheehy,[29] and *Spiritual Development* by Daniel Helminiak.[30] And of course the granddaddy of them all is Erik Erikson's chapter "Eight Ages of Man" in his foundational *Childhood and Society.*[31]

One final study suggestion: As a pastoral psychotherapist I found that I needed a way to think about people who said they felt spiritual but not religious, at least not religious in terms of their life-long worship communities. They often said that they didn't "fit," yet they wished, even yearned, for a satisfying way of expressing their spiritual natures. In response to this recurring issue, and drawing on the work of Urban T. Holmes, I developed a way to determine and describe "spiritual type." Just as we have temperamental types, as seen in using the MBTI, so we have spiritual types, inclining us to express ourselves in one of four basic ways, spiritually. The book explaining these spiritual types is *Discover*

Your Spiritual Type, and it includes a basic testing instrument, designed for Protestants and evangelicals, plus one for Roman Catholics and one for Jews, each with a slightly altered vocabulary fitting those worship patterns.[32]

As I present this typology I find that people are fascinated by discovering their spiritual type and exploring what this means about how they best respond to God. The book also allows readers to determine the spiritual type most favored by their worshipping congregation and then compare how well matched the church or synagogue is to a particular reader's individual type. Suggestions are made about directions for growth, how to supplement congregational experience with practices that enhance individual spiritual needs, and how to relate to others whose spirituality may be quite different from one's own. The book is easy to read. No great theological or psychological background is needed to understand these descriptions of differing spiritualities.

Prayer and Scripture

You will notice that this chapter does not have a separate Bible Study heading. That is for two reasons. First, I trust that your church provides ongoing opportunities for the study of scripture. This is especially critical for those who did not grow up with the biblical stories as templates for shaping their personal value systems. Many churches offer such classes, and adding a Bible study plan here would be redundant to the many plans already developed for that purpose. Second, in keeping with the purpose of a spiritual formation group, I here suggest a very different way of doing scripture reading, one that emphasizes not study or knowledge, but instead focuses on what God may be saying to us as we meditate on a passage. The approach used here will combine scripture reading and prayer into one integrated experience. For those who have chosen Bible study as their exclusive area of interest, this alternative way of "praying the scriptures" may be especially useful.

Prayer may be a separate study of its own, of course. The section on prayer in the preceding chapter is a good starting place for this study. Read especially the resources noted in the endnotes for chapter 4. These particular books were selected because they are good ones for beginning study. That does not mean they can be read through quickly. They are meant to serve as a survey of the field, and a way to get you started. When you find yourself particularly drawn to a certain aspect of the study, follow up on that book's bibliography.

Not covered in the prayer section of chapter 4 is a discussion of two distinct ways of praying with scriptural images, the Ignatian way and *lectio divina*. These two approaches can provide deeply spiritual experiences through reading and prayerfully meditating on scripture.

The Ignatian Way

A classic in Christian literature, *The Spiritual Exercises of Ignatius of Loyola* was written in 1533 as the framework of a four-week meditative retreat. There are many translations of the Ignatian exercises available. The endnotes cite a paperback version that includes a brief biography.[33] The exercises are interesting to review as a historical piece, and they give a taste of what a disciplined Jesuit retreat is like. I like to recommend this way of praying to people who want things to be very specific and spelled-out. Ignatius tells you exactly what to do. Even if you are one who feels the exercises are too directive and arbitrary, just reading them will give you a taste of the rigorous prayer patterns followed by practitioners. One interpreter of the Ignatian exercises has called them a spiritual marathon. Taking one exercise and actually doing it (following the directions) will better inform the group about the Ignatian way of praying with images. Ignatius himself urged that the exercises be adapted to convenient use. A contemporary and slightly more flexible version of the Ignatian exercises has been developed by James W. Skehan and is available in the book *Place Me with Your Son*.[34]

In all the exercises the participant is asked to dwell on the persons, the words, and the actions of a Gospel text suggested by Ignatius. After reading the scripture passage, there are stages of prayer through which one progresses, each stage leading more deeply into peaceful and receptive prayer, until finally the participant is totally immersed into the mystery of Christ's life. This last stage is called the "application of the senses" because, in a passive way, we are to see, smell, hear, and feel ourselves "into" the story of the text. Both Ignatian prayer and *lectio divina* guide the one who prays toward immersing the imagination in the text. The *Spiritual Exercises* do so in a detailed and more structured way, using assigned scripture passages.

Lectio Divina

Compare Ignatius' approach with the more accessible and deeply trans-
formational *lectio divina* ("sacred reading") method designed for "praying the scriptures." This is a shorter process, one adapted to, say, fifteen
to thirty minutes at a sitting. This method was used as early as the fourth
and fifth centuries, and because of its effectiveness, it has never gone out
of favor. Using this approach, you will not be studying scripture as does
an academic or a scholar, but you will engage the text in a meditative,
prayerful attitude, which is quite different.

Ask the members to begin by choosing a brief passage of scripture
for the group and reading through it quietly four times, each time seeing
it through different eyes and from a different point of view. This can be
done silently or aloud by a reader. First, read the text selection to just
"get into" the passage, to imagine being at the scene, or entering into the
author's concerns. Second, ask yourself some questions about the passage: Why is it included in the scripture record? What meaning does
this passage have for me, and how does it affect my understanding of
God? The third reading is for acknowledging feelings about the passage.
Did you find it dull? Did it make you angry or relieved or happy? This
opens the way for you to talk to God (to pray) about what you have experienced from your reading. Last, after the fourth reading, sit in quietness before God, letting your focus and attention be on the passage,
listening with your heart. This is the most difficult part for most of us.

The "how to" of it is carefully explained by the writers of both the
books I recommend here: I suggest two among many sources and I
choose these for their easy-to-read presentations. The first is chapter 3
in a book previously cited, *Prayer and Temperament* by Michael and
Norrisey.[35] The book refers to the Myers Briggs temperament types and
connects this to the way we go about praying. The other book is my own
Discover Your Spiritual Type.[36] In chapter 8 I explain how *lectio divina*
meets the needs of all personality and spirituality types. The chapter
explains exactly how to go through a brief passage of scripture in this
meditative way. Especially useful is page 107, a condensed guide for
following the *lectio* format.

Because of damaging past experiences, many seekers find scripture
reading uninteresting, irrelevant, even threatening. They may have been
verbally shamed by people who reinforced the abuse by quoting out-of-
context biblical warnings. For those interested in recovering their

appreciation of scripture, lectio divina may be the answer, and it does make a fine, experiential group study.

Traditions and Their Spiritualities

One could easily choose to study the traditions of various faiths, and a popular book by Huston Smith is a good beginning for that study.[37] An investigation of Jewish spirituality, the ground from which Christianity rises, would also be interesting to many Christians. (For a start on such a study, get Milton Steinberg's little paperback *Basic Judaism*[38] or Abraham Heschel's *God in Search of Man: A Philosophy of Judaism*.[39])

The focus of the spiritual formation group presented here will not be on learning about comparative religions, but on learning about various faith groups within Christianity. That is something of great interest when we visit the worship services of friends, attend funerals and special occasions, or meet people from congregations other than our own and ask, "Why do they do it that way?" A wonderful new book, *How to Be a Perfect Stranger*, is a guide to etiquette when visiting other people's religious services and ceremonies.[40] It reviews twenty different worshipping groups, includes a brief synopsis of their beliefs, and clues you in on how to conduct yourself in their services. It will be a help in the study of each denomination and is a good selection for your church library. (I understand that a second, companion volume is to be published soon.) This book will be essential as group members visit other worshipping communities. James F. White's *Protestant Worship: Traditions in Transition* goes a bit deeper, furnishing a review of current trends in Protestant worship and beliefs.[41] For an overview of 220 different denominations, see the tenth edition of Frank Mead's *Handbook of Denominations in the United States*.[42]

To approach this sort of project, various people in the group might look into a particular Christian worship tradition and present to the group what they have discovered about the spirituality of that community. One may choose a tradition with which she has some connection, possibly a familial or educational (alma mater) connection. Another may choose a tradition that puzzles him. A Southern Baptist friend of mine recently attended an Episcopal funeral service and said she wished she could have better understood the meaning of what was going on. If this sort of open, inquiring attitude characterizes those in your spiritual formation group, participants may find this to be an interesting and very broadening study. It can also result in some group members learning to stand even more firmly on their own theological ground. Here are some traditions that make for interesting inquiry.

Roman Catholic Spirituality

There are about nine hundred million members of the Roman Catholic Church, sixty million in the United States. Not learning about Catholicism would be, at the very least, a gross oversight. The first thing to do, of course, is to attend a Roman Catholic Mass. If you are not Roman Catholic, you will not be invited to receive Communion, although it is very appropriate for you to stand, sit, kneel, read prayers (if you wish), and sing with the congregation. Enter into the service to the greatest degree that you can, and see if you can pick up the flavor of this sacramental style of worship. How is it different from your own experience? What is being emphasized, and what are the most important moments in the worship service? What most attracts you? Puzzles you? Repels you?

Suggested reading sources are *Essentials of the Faith,*[43] an easy-to-read interpretation of the Catholic catechism, *Why Do Catholics Do That?*[44] a book about customs and rituals, and *A Concise History of the Catholic Church.*[45] An internet home page at http://www.catholic.com gives information about worship practices, current activities, policy positions, and general information. Almost every denomination now has a home page for browsing, and using the keyword method is a good way to search.

Lutheran and Reformation Spiritualities

The Protestant Reformation was a watershed within the life of Christianity, an event and an outcome about which we must know if we are to appreciate this unique spiritual legacy. The name *Protestant* was given to sixteenth-century protesters against Roman Catholicism. The movement was and remains characterized by acceptance of the Bible as the sole source of revealed truth, the doctrine of justification by faith only, and the priesthood of all believers, meaning that believers have direct access to God. These beliefs are usually set out in statements called creeds or confessions. In a Protestant worship service, preaching is more prominent than the liturgical elements of more sacramental faiths such as Roman Catholicism, Anglicanism, and Eastern Orthodoxy. Although they follow the Reformed tradition, Baptists and Methodists are treated separately here because of their unique histories and subsequent differences.

Present-day Protestantism is chiefly the legacy of Martin Luther, John Calvin, and Ulrich Zwingli. There are two main Lutheran denominations active in the United States: the Evangelical Lutheran Church in America (ELCA) and the more conservative Lutheran Church—Missouri Synod. Like the Roman Catholic service, Lutheran worship is liturgical, but the service is simpler and, like most Protestant denominations, emphasizes the preaching activity. Check to see if you can take Communion. It is likely that nonmembers will not be permitted to receive. You may participate in everything else and will probably find something familiar to you, as Lutheranism expresses both sacramental and evangelical strands of worship.

The other major denomination within the Reform tradition is the Presbyterian Church which is found throughout the United States. The Reformed Church of America is a denomination primarily prevalent on the East Coast. Smaller Reformed groups include the United Church of Christ and the Disciples of Christ.

You might check out Luther's *The Small Catechism*.[46] A helpful commentary is found in *Reformed Spirituality* by Howard L. Rice. I especially resonated with Rice's comment that "Reformed Protestants developed another form of spiritual direction, the group."[47] He talks about prayer, study, and the experience of God found in the Reformed churches.

A fine book for several of these denominational studies is *Protestant Spiritual Traditions*.[48] Although the book does not deal specifically with denominations, Reformed spirituality is well explained, especially through a chapter on the spirituality of John Calvin.

For an inspirational approach, read *The Cost of Discipleship* by Dietrich Bonhoeffer.[49] A member of the Confessing Church formed in Germany during Nazi rule, Bonhoeffer opposed Hitler and was imprisoned and executed. Here is a Reformed spirituality lived out under the most trying circumstances; the book is a "must read" for this inquiry.

Anglican Spirituality

In the United States, members of the worldwide Anglican Communion are called Episcopalians, members of the Episcopal Church. It is thought of as being both formally liturgical and informally inclusive. Babies are welcome, even if they cry, and theological variations are tolerated, but within certain limits. For example, nonmembers are welcome to take Communion, but only if they are baptized. The vocabulary is decidedly English; the church basement is even called the undercroft.

Anglicanism is a peculiar mixture of the mystical, the intellectual, and the practical, a combination that appeals to many. Modern writers such as Dorothy Sayers, C. S. Lewis, T. S. Eliot, and J. R. R. Tolkien exemplify this ambiguity of intellect and mystery so characteristic of the Anglican mind. Anglicanism is said to have a feminine consciousness, which is to say that it can acknowledge darkness as well as light. For this reason it is not a confessional church with the clear-cut certainties that formal confessional statements imply. Anglicans do, however, recite in their liturgy one of the three ancient creeds of the Christian church, the Apostles' Creed, the Nicene Creed, or the Athanasian Creed.

The best introduction to the Episcopal Church is, happily, the most entertaining: *What Is Anglicanism?* by Urban T. Holmes.[50] It is a fairly short explanation of biblical views, doctrinal stands, liturgy, and corporate spirituality. *Evangelicals on the Canterbury Trail* by Robert Webber explains the appeal of Anglicanism to those who come into it from other traditions.[51] *What Makes Us Episcopalians* by John Booty is also a good resource.[52] I have written a booklet called *What Is Liturgy?* which is designed to help the non-Episcopal visitor make sense of what is going on in the worship service.[53] It is designed to be put into those tract racks that seem to be in every Episcopal church foyer. Larger Episcopal churches frequently have bookstores on the premises, and you will usually find good material of all types of the kind needed by a spiritual formation group. As you see, to be Anglican is to be a reader.

Eastern Orthodox Spirituality

In the United States, a Greek or Russian Orthodox church is not as common as the churches of other traditions we have discussed. They are well worth the search, however, and you will learn much about this deeply felt spirituality from simply being in the worship services. Try very hard to disconnect from your logical, rational mind; this is a worship pattern and an architecture that evokes mystery and majesty. Particularly notice the art displayed on walls, altar, and especially the ceiling. Sight, smell, and touch all blend to evoke a most affecting experience. Communion is offered in a way untypical of Western churches. Check with the usher to see if nonmembers are allowed to receive. Most often outsiders are not.

There are some very good writers in this tradition, and even the scholarly books are inspirational. *The Orthodox Way* by Kallistos (Timothy) Ware will give you most of what you need to understand Eastern spirituality.[54] Another representative work is *For the Life of the World: Sacraments and Orthodoxy* by Alexander Schmemann.[55] And to get the feel of the Russian Orthodox Church from a historical point of view, rent a video of *Young Catherine*, a well-made film that tells the story of Catherine the Great including her conversion to the Russian Orthodox Church. (You may wish to review the film before running it for anyone under sixteen.)

Some Other Spiritualities

The groups covered in this subheading are not dumped into a single category because they are less important. Indeed, these traditions have influence and weight, and much is written about them. They are, however, quite individual spiritualities, some partaking of other major traditions, but, still, uniquely their own.

Methodists are clearly the spiritual legacy of a single man, John Wesley. I can do no better than to quote David Lowes Watson when he says that Wesley's "genius was to create a theological synthesis between the two major strands of English Protestant spirituality—Anglican holiness of intent and Puritan inward assurance—and apply it in the practical outworking of an accountable discipleship."[56] Watson's chapter "Methodist Spirituality" is very worth reading. A more detailed treatment is found in *John and Charles Wesley: Selected Writings and Hymns* by Frank Whaling.[57] The quick and cheap way to acquaint yourself with Methodism is to get the fine little book often given to new members, *The*

United Methodist Way.[58] It gives a taste of the history, beliefs, and organization of this influential denomination. A recent treatment is the paperback *Living Our Beliefs,* which will give you the most up-to-date explanations of the Methodist ethos.[59] If you have never before been in a Methodist worship service, my guess is that you will notice how comfortable it feels to be there. You will be invited to take Communion; if you do, the assumption is that you are a professing Christian.

As for Baptists, the largest groups are the National Baptists (African American), the Southern Baptists, and the American Baptists.

White visitors will feel warmly welcomed in a National Baptist congregation. The spirituality is deeply felt and contagious. The singing is magnificent, and the preaching delivery is often reminiscent of that powerful speaking style characteristic of so many contemporary civil rights leaders. A book that explores the historical roots of African American religious expression is *The Spirituality of African American Peoples* by Peter Paris.[60] I also recommend *Deep River and Negro Spirituality* by Howard Thurman.[61] There are other scholarly books written about African American spirituality, but nothing substitutes for the experience of it.

Southern Baptist life is in an uproar right now, partially because their churches are autonomous; each congregation is accountable only to itself, and of course to God as they interpret God. Do not be distracted or put off by this moderate versus conservative quarrel. There is much to learn from Baptist tradition about a vigorous and independent spirituality. In their worship services, preaching is central, with music a close second. Theirs is not what we call a liturgical church, but there is a clear order in the worship, nonetheless. There are several good histories about Southern Baptists, but in the light of current changes within the denomination, it might be best to ask for or to order the most recent pamphlets published by the Southern Baptist Historical Society.[62] These pamphlets cover subjects such as the history of Baptists, their central beliefs, and their important role in the issue of separation of church and state which arose during America's early formation as a democracy. A book written recently, and aware of the changes, is *The Baptist Way of Life* by Brooks Hayes and John Steely.[63] A long-used standard is *A History of the Baptists* by Robert G. Torbet.[64]

A unique spirituality is now emerging in what is being called the megachurch—enormous congregations with ground-hugging contemporary buildings that have little or no denominational signage. There are multitudes of programs, and state-of-the-art sight and sound equipment. I suggest group members visit and experience what is so appealing to a growing number of previously unchurched people. Here you have a blending of American marketing techniques with a strong evangelical Christianity. They carry out Paul's statement in his first letter to the Corinthians, admonishing them to be "all things to all" in order to save "some." They emphasize the Word as found in scripture, as well as the gospel according to Peter Drucker, among others. These are churches to take seriously. To get a summary of the movement and its gurus, read the feature article "The Next Church" in the August 1996 issue of *Atlantic Monthly.*

Any number of denominations and independent congregations could be categorized as fundamentalists. Dramatic preaching is usually central to the worship service, with a focus on the literal interpretation of scripture, and sometimes the practice of public healings or revelations from God. Music is uncomplicated, rhythmic, and often high decibel. Some of these groups are not affiliated with a denomination; some are. The best way to learn about them is to visit a worship service or a revival meeting. The intensity of feeling and participation may surprise you; it may also help to explain the attraction that an increasing number of people have to this spontaneous spirituality. One good book that explains the movement is George Marsden's *Understanding Fundamentalism and Evangelicalism.*[65] Because fundamentalist groups are influential in the lives of many Americans, it is important to understand this spirituality.

Feminist Spirituality

For those who especially want to look into the recent and significant contributions of women to spirituality, theology, and biblical interpretation, the field is rich in reading material. For beginners I suggest a book called *She Who Is: The Mystery of God in Feminist Theological Discourse* by Elizabeth A. Johnson.[66] The book is not only a recent and nicely balanced presentation of feminist thought, but it also provides quotations and references from other major contributors to the field. This one book will be your passport to others you may enjoy. If you wish to go further, a comprehensive guide is the many authored *Dictionary of Feminist Theologies*, a reference reviewing the last thirty years of feminist theology, plus entries about every kind of feminist theological issue.[67] Whether you do or do not agree with all you learn about feminist theology, it is important that you become exposed to what has become a major movement in our time. Many writers report a change in their experience of God as a result of heightened feminist awareness, and it is important that students of the spiritual life understand the difference that a feminist interpretation places on spirituality.

Historic Doctrines of the Church

As a change of pace, try looking at the question "What do we believe and how on earth did this belief come about?" You will be amazed at how the politics and mores of a particular time influenced the outcome of what we now unquestioningly accept as fixed doctrine. You will come away from this study with more conviction about some doctrines and less about others. Is that scary?

For the study of this topic I make a one-book recommendation that will lead you to other books which may interest you: *A Short History of Christian Thought* by Linwood Urban, revised in 1995.[68] Although the paperback version is 461 pages long, the text on any one subject is concise and brief and not difficult to read. The book's length is accounted for by the wide range of topics covered. Urban provides a good view of both the "forest and the trees," meaning he gives a good survey of the entire landscape.

If all of the members of the spiritual formation group are communicants of the same denomination, you may wish to also use that denomination's doctrinal books as added resources. Your clergy or a divinity school professor might make suggestions for group study. Be sure and ask for an easy-to-read, beginning text.

And Much More

There are almost endless topics for consideration as study projects. You will come across them as you tackle other studies, and soon will have at hand more interests than the group can handle. But be sure you stay close to the group's intention which is toward spiritual growth. A study on self-esteem, habits of successful people, or making a will is not appropriate for this particular group, worthy as those topics may be. (Chapter 6 will make suggestions about how to keep a discussion focused on spiritual life.) The fortunate thing about the study of spirituality is that new sources and new inner experiences keep fueling the seeker who persists. My guess is that, once engaged, you will not ever again complain of life having no meaning. In an authentically spiritual life, there is always more meaning than we can manage!

CHAPTER 6

Sharing the Journey

(In response to Descartes "Cogito ergo sum": I think, therefore I am):

It is not the individual's capacity to think which is the prime source of his or her identity formation, but rather the reality and the ability of belonging, participating, and sharing. The sharing of one's life with another's leads to wholeness and guarantees health.
                                                    Musamba Ma Mpolo

After several months together, and learning of the struggles and victories present in each life, the group becomes a context of caring and common concern. It becomes "the home away from home." As we share (have a part in the lives of others), we become willing to speak the truth about our lives and God's interaction with us. Making a time for exchanging experiences of the spiritual journey enhances self-discovery and provides mutual support.

So what shall the group talk about in this forty-minute segment? Two areas of experience will furnish more than enough subject matter: (1) a personal application made of the study just presented and (2) the life events in each person's experience that affect spiritual growth. So take five, get your coffee, stretch your legs, and come back to settle in for the time of "sharing the journey."

Focusing on the Study

There will occasionally be a desire to reflect further on how the study just presented has impact on personal attitude and spirituality. Let's say someone presented a study of another religious tradition including a personal visit to that group's worship service. After the forty to forty-five minutes allotted to the study activity, all may agree that the sharing time should be used to allow members to respond personally to what was presented. Some may want to comment on their own interior experience of worship in a particular setting. How were they affected by aspects of the service? What was going on not just in the congregation but in them?

The developmental study may prompt some discussion of what different members have noticed to be characteristic of their ongoing spiritual lives. Many subjects bear additional discussion of a more subjective type. Note that during the time of sharing the discussion should shift to the personal, not be academic. Study is a head-trip; sharing is a heart-trip.

Focusing on Life Events

Most often the group will want to focus on things within their own lives that are affecting their understanding of God or their closeness to and distance from God. As we talk about our life events, we are able to participate in the spiritual journey with others. A life event, it should be said, can be either a circumstance that happens to us (from the outside) or an inner transition or change. One way to open conversation is for the convener to ask, "What has happened in your world recently that has made a difference in your spiritual life?"

This conversation may be the most nourishing part of the group's interaction. It also has a pitfall, a way in which things can get off track. Without being too strict about what is off limits, the spiritual formation group is not primarily a problem-solving or psychoanalytical effort. It is a gathering focused on present-moment spiritual growth. This focus must be kept clearly in mind. There is no way, of course, that problem solving or looking into one's past patterns and how they affect the present can be excluded from any discussion of personal spirituality.

Our problems and our pasts greatly affect what goes on within us now. But exploring the present, daily spiritual quest takes priority, and this is the group's primary purpose.

How, then, can things be kept on track, while respecting the needs expressed? We can retain the focus if we persist in asking some important questions. One question to ask of anyone's story is "Where do you see God working in all this?" How does what one has just said reveal activity or interaction with God? What do we suppose can come out of the event? Or consider this question: "Where are you now, and where are you going?" We "come to clarity" about ourselves and an event as we receive feedback from the group. Group response serves as a mirror held up to reflect the shifts and changes, even the crises, we experience. Feedback is an important component of what some call the art of discernment.

Sharing Effectively

Psychotherapists training to conduct groups are often given an aptly titled book by William Friedman, *How to Do Groups*.[1] It is designed specifically for therapy groups. Although I have referenced it in the endnotes, I am not suggesting that its information is appropriate for a spiritual formation group. However, Friedman's chapter "What to Focus on during a Group Therapy Session" contains an invaluable piece of wisdom, which I think applies here. Friedman's important message is that the group should focus on the here-and-now rather than on the there-and-then. Group work is best done when there is attention to the moment. In the case of a therapy group, this would mean attention to the interaction of members with one another. In the case of a spiritual formation group, I would refocus this tact to refer to this question: "What is going on with you spiritually, *right now?*" Participants will, of course, need to say something about their spiritual histories; how they once perceived God, the path taken in their evolving relationships with God, or perhaps the things they were taught that they now question. But the growing edge for each one will be to communicate to the group the things that are happening to them currently. How are their lives changing? What new thoughts and experiences are they having? Has anyone in the group had an experience that parallels what has been related by another? How did they deal with those changes? Sharing the journey means just that: We offer what we know and help when we can.

Welcoming the Stranger

The stranger is one who is new to us or is unlike us. Not everyone coming to the spiritual formation group will be known to other members or will be like them in faith and convictions. "Doubt is sometimes a codeword [meaning] a defect in religious faith. . . ." says Robert Lovinger.[2] How will the group feel toward those who express doubts concerning religious beliefs or experiences? A spiritual formation group is an appropriate place for someone serious about faith, despite grave doubts. It would be a shame if, on hearing a seeker's religious questions, group members decided the doubter was not "suitable" for a gathering devoted to spiritual growth. What better place to be than with people who also care about the God connection?

Doubt is not an indicator of religious failure. Rather, it is often that quality that most informs an intelligent and thoughtful future faith. If the inquiry leads to deeper doubt or to different views, then that is where it leads. *Group members are not in charge of managing a particular outcome.* We say, after all, that God is powerful, and that God's Spirit is able to work in each person. We should trust that power and not make the mistake of becoming controllers, implying that only we, not God, can act in creation. Our job is to form a context of caring. We may be very surprised at what God wants, and the zigzag path that leads to it.

In commenting on why groups fail, two experts say that "the conflict between individual and group goals is often the reason why some groups can't get off the ground."[3] If the goal is to find people who think and believe exactly alike, the nonconformist will not be welcome. If, however, the goal is to grow in one's capacity to relate to the Holy, then that goal will embrace any members who are also interested in how, and even if, they can relate to a power higher than themselves. If their goal is to irritate and to interfere with the group's goal, that is another matter, and the facilitator will have to make clear to them the group's purposes.

We Grow in Community

The spiritual formation group will be greatly enriched if the views of one are not uniformly held by another. If two can present differing viewpoints in a respectful and listening manner, wider horizons for each appear. How would you know who you were, if you didn't know who you weren't? I can imagine nothing more dehumanizing, actually un-human, than a world full of creatures who perfectly and identically resembled each other. How would one identify oneself or anyone else? We learn by contrasting one concept with another; we learn from the difference!

For some, difficulties in participating will not be about agreement or disagreement with other members. Rather, difficulties will involve their reticence in revealing their lives to others. We must not insist, as many do, "Oh, go ahead and talk; no one will mind!" If members are hesitant to share, that is entirely their business. Let them sit and listen. It is like-ly they will share their story as they become more comfortable. If they never do, that is okay. Any group leader can tell you about some indi-vidual who remains silent, even expressionless, during every group session, only to reveal at the end that he benefited in life-changing ways from being a part of the group. Convincing everyone to share equally is not the goal here. Growth and insight are the goals, and each person must attend to that in her own way.

Group members who participate readily feel fairly unthreatened, possibly because they have been in sharing groups before. You can de-pend on having several such people who will help to get things started until more join in. The sense of safety is an important issue. Members who come to understand that each is there to support the other will, in time, feel more liberty to speak. We cannot know the situation from which anyone else comes. The spiritual formation group may be the only setting in which some people feel acceptance and safety—whether or not they do much talking.

We may question the value of trying to pursue our own spiritual growth while interacting with others. There is a type of solitary spiritual life that is called the anchoritic or eremetical life, where the individual has become a recluse, or hermit, to seek God. Few people are called to this vocation, and if they are, it is no blessing if their retreat is only for the purpose of escape. The true eremetic is one who has long interacted with others and has thoroughly worked out her own sense of self and vocational calling. All of us must begin in community; only in relating to each other can we do most of our growing.

Another type of spiritual life, called the cenobitic life, is done by one who chooses to live in community as the path to deeper spirituality. One of the studies suggested in chapter 7 is on the Benedictine rule. Benedict, with great wisdom, insisted that for his monks spiritual growth must take place in community; each person is required to live out the spiritual life in the natural friction caused by interacting with others. There are many potentially growth-producing communities: couples, families, churches, organizations of all sorts. A spiritual formation group must be exactly that—forming one's spiritual life. Its value is that it serves as a matrix for maturity, especially spiritual maturity. The psalmist agrees: "Happy are the people . . . whose hearts are set on the pilgrims' way" (84:4).[4]

CHAPTER 7

Making a "Rule"

"Religionizing" only one part of life secularizes the rest of it.
Abraham Maslow

This chapter is included so that the spiritual formation group will consider making this activity first a study and then an individual practice. It is not suggested as a group-meeting activity because it is a daily pattern, lived out privately as each member chooses. The group can engage in a study using the resources suggested, and then encourage each member in creating or adapting an individualized rule. From time to time, during the sharing part of the meetings, members may comment on particular experiences of living out their chosen daily patterns, or "rule," as I am calling it here.

Rule is a medieval word for *a specific daily pattern for maintaining spiritual awareness.* Many well-known rules have been practiced in the past, and new versions are now being developed by religious groups of all kinds. You can establish your own pattern, as have many people before you. Claude Payne, Episcopal bishop of the Diocese of Texas, recalls that his grandfather, whom he loved and admired, "prayed every night in an audible whisper as part of his rule of life."[1] Later, in his own life, Payne was influenced to maintain a regular prayer time of his own, remembering how impressed he was by the daily practice of his grandfather.

In a letter John Wesley exhorted a friend, "O, Begin! Fix some part of every day for private exercises . . . else you will be a trifler all your days. . . . Do not starve yourself any longer."[2] Good advice!

Patterns in the Past

Structuring one's day to spiritual ends is an ancient practice. One biblical scholar notes that at the time of Jesus, Judaism marked each day in the Jerusalem temple with morning and evening sacrifices and with services of psalms and prayers at 9 A.M. and 3 P.M.[3] An ancient practice among devout Jews was to pray privately morning, noon, and again at the close of day (see Ps. 55:17). Some scholars believe that synagogues in the larger Palestinian towns had daily morning and evening services. In addition to prayer, the reading of scriptures had a central part in Jewish corporate worship.

We have evidence that Christians followed this daily pattern as early as the second century, though probably earlier, gathering both morning and evening for prayer and reading. Christian private prayer later followed the pattern of morning, noon, and night and, in time, more hours for devotion were added.[4] Latin terms such as *matins, lauds, vespers,* and *compline* named these meditational hours. Later, a type of book for the laity, *The Book of Hours*, was developed, hand lettered and beautifully illuminated. These pages took the reader easily through a day's or week's prayers and readings. A fine collection of these exquisite volumes can be seen in the British Museum.

The best known rule is that of Saint Benedict written in 540 C.E. for his lay monks. Benedict drew from patterns previously worked out by other spiritual masters and crafted for his own monastic community a daily schedule that, when adapted to modern life, is still a practical and effective tool for staying spiritually connected. To oversimplify, Benedict's rule consists of guidelines for *work, study, community*, and *prayer*. Were we to adapt this simple formula to our own lives, what could we devise?

The Benedictine emphasis on work, study, community, and prayer implies that all of life faces Godward. Indeed, a rule is by definition a plan for "ruling" all one's life to this end. For example, Benedict saw *work* as a gift to God, rather than as drudgery or self-interest. (We also come to understand that work is not the most important component of life.) For Benedict *study* was a way of internalizing scripture and the writings of the church fathers. His emphasis on being in a stable *community* can be met, in some measure, through the church and particularly in the interaction and support present in the spiritual formation group.

And last, a rule is most associated in our minds with daily times of *prayer*. Actually, this careful working out of work, study, community, and prayer, which might now be called a "lifestyle" rather than a rule, is a practical approach to living a more stress-free and God-connected life while being immersed in contemporary society. When approached in this simple way, a rule is not intimidating, indeed, it is a peaceful and responsible enrichment to life, providing the grounding framework for each day.

Creating Your Own Rule

Creating a personal pattern, a rule for one's life, is something any group member will need to consider carefully. If you were living in a disciplined community, such as a monastic order, these decisions would be imposed on you by your choice of that order. Most of us do not live in such a community, and therefore we must consider what actually will work in our own lives. What is realistic and doable for you as an individual? Ask yourself, "How can work, study, community, and prayer be done with my time, and in my time?"

Work

We generally think of work as being outside the realm of the spiritual. We may acknowledge that our business ethics and interactions with others are to be governed by Christian principles and biblical commandments, but we seldom think of the work itself as a way of relating to God. Were we to follow a Benedictine point of view, we would see work as much more than income earning. Even the most menial tasks, such as the washing of dishes, Benedict regarded as service to others and, as such, holy. In the little classic *The Practice of the Presence of God*, Brother Lawrence says of his companions that "our sanctification did not depend upon changing our works, but in doing that for God's sake which we commonly do for our own."[5] If what we do contributes in any way to the restoration of order, of happiness, of fulfillment and wholeness in others and in ourselves, we do the work of God in the world! The key is in seeing work as contributing, not simply as making a living. Ministry is not the preserve of only some but the call of all. Our work is an essential part of our greater call, our effort at *tikkun ha'olam*, a Hebrew phrase meaning "to heal (or to repair) the world."

Seeing work as holy forces us to ask some difficult questions. Does what I do for a living help or harm? Is what I say simple and truthful? Do those who work with me feel uplifted or diminished—are they calmer or more stressed—by my presence? Do I accomplish the work for which I am paid? Do I share my gains with others who have need? The lived-out answers to these questions make a difference in the world; indeed, our work tends to tear down or to build up the creation. As you walk into your place of work, pray that your efforts will "heal the world" a bit that day. As you leave for home or other places, review the day and ask God to bless the work you have done. Approaching work as contribution makes it holy.

Study

Study was a component of Benedictine life. We have also incorporated it into the spiritual formation group session, acknowledging it as an essential and necessary part of spiritual growth. Group members may come to have very different ideas about what should be studied by the group and/or individually, but I trust they will agree that study of some sort contributes to broadening one's view of what is possible. The medieval monks called their study "spiritual reading," and they, of course, were limited to what they had available in readable form. But they knew it made a difference in their lives, forming their minds and spirits toward a larger life.

Privately, group members may wish to read each day from the Book of Psalms or the gospels, or from a spiritually related book or article, choosing something that will contribute enrichment to the day. Reading may be relevant to the current topic being studied by the group. Structure your reading to fit your life. If something that is supposed to be "good" bores or irritates you, give it a fair try and then put it aside. You may be ready for it later, or you may just decide it is not your style of stuff. In planning for individual time, a mixture of scripture and reading, even hymn texts and poems, can freshen your interest.

Group members might like to follow the format of books of daily readings that include prayers, comments, and scripture quotations, such as the Job and Shawchuck volumes suggested in chapter 5. Several denominational presses print booklets arranged so that devotional material with related scripture passages are presented for each day. The only warning I make about these denominational publications is their tendency to offer writing that is short and easy, when what you may want is a more sustained treatment with added spiritual depth. The short-and-easy approach is fine for those who choose it, but group members who are looking for significant spiritual growth may require more.

Your priest or pastor has probably been trained in a theological seminary, a place that offers a very bookish kind of education. His or her bookshelves will be filled with a variety of reading. I don't suggest you borrow books, but a theologically educated person is invaluable in guiding you to whole areas of inquiry. There is no reason *at all* that theological education should be confined to people seeking ordination. Are we not all "theological"?

The endnotes of each chapter in this book serve as a resource for reading; books cited are especially selected for reasonably easy and nourishing reading.

Finally, I suggest group members and conveners get on the mailing lists of a few of the many book distributors and publishers that specialize in religious books and sell through direct-mail channels. Most of these mail out small, free catalogs showing both the best-selling books and those that have been recently published. As you know, once you order anything from one of them, you get on other related mailing lists. The book you are now reading is published by The Alban Institute, specializing in books that help develop congregational life. You can call them (see back of book for 800 number) to request a copy of their catalog. I also suggest, as a start, the Religious Book Club[6] (it is excellent and you don't have to "join" to order or get a discount) or any of the Cokesbury catalogs.[7] These two offer an assortment of titles from many publishers. See the endnotes for some additional catalog sources from individual publishers.[8] Just knowing what is being written in the fields of religion and spirituality—reading the book descriptions—is a fascinating part of what you can learn.

Setting aside a time for reading each day or regularly during the week is challenging. It is important to remember that covering a certain amount of material has nothing to do with the purpose of what the

Benedictines called spiritual reading. The focus is not on how much is read but on what it does for the reader. In your reading you may come across a small paragraph that is so right for your needs that you stop and think about it, reading no further.

It is also important not to have as a goal spending a certain amount of time on reading. Ideally, you may choose to set aside an hour or just fifteen minutes for yourself, but reading for exactly that long is not the point. The goal of spiritual reading is that it nourishes and contributes to your spiritual understanding.

Some members who are early risers will read in the morning. A friend of mine said that if she gave God her early morning hours, she would be offering the worst time of her day. She chooses afternoons, because she is more alert then, and it fits her schedule. A pastor I know sets aside time on weekends for longer reading, using only very short meditations for weekday use. Each of these people is intentional about reserving time, whenever and for however long. It is very much like deciding to begin an exercise program. You choose the way you need to exercise, the time of day you will devote to it, and how long you will work out. But the purpose is not just to say you did it; it is to strengthen your body. Just so, spiritual reading strengthens the spirit.

Community

Several nights ago I watched the 1984 film *Greystoke: The Legend of Tarzan, Lord of the Apes*. I have heard that the Tarzan story has been made into a movie twenty-eight times. I can't verify that, but it is clear that the story of a man being brought up by apes is endlessly fascinating. Most of us sense that we learn of ourselves through interaction with others. What, we ask, would it have been like to be reared by a community of apes, with no human reference? In *Tarzan* we see the ape man return to human society, and we anguish with him as he finds himself to be emotionally inept and intellectually incompatible.

All this is to say that it matters very much that we live in community. It affects who we become! Were you reared in the South? Are you black, white, or brown skinned? What does it matter? It matters in that we come to understand the world in terms of the attitudes and habits of the people who surrounded us. I have noticed a difference in those formed within certain church communities; there is also a difference in those who have grown up without a worshipping community. This is not a good/bad evaluation, but an observation that who we become is greatly influenced by who is there for us when we have questions.

A group gathered for the purpose of growing spiritually will have an influence on each person in it. If the group values prayer, and prayer is experienced and talked about by the members, then prayer will be on the minds of members; they will be more likely to develop a prayer life than people whose group values are, say, financial profitability or physical fitness, not that either is a negative value. I'm simply saying that the social contexts of our lives form us. Spiritual formation is best done among those who value it. Selecting community is a part of one's personal rule of life.

The Benedictines stress what their founder called stability. Benedict was among the first to suggest that staying in one place, geographically, was a good thing. Other orders of monks typically wandered about through cities and countryside, as they moved asking alms from the faithful. Benedict believed that work and self-supporting communities—stability—were conducive to spiritual growth.

As a society, we even now wander across the land in response to job opportunities, although there is new effort by companies not to uproot families quite so often. As we move, we seek our stability within the corporation itself or in some organization that promotes our particular interests. We also find it in churches. In almost every situation we enter, if we look, we can find a cluster of people who are thirsty for more of the experience of God. Community is very deep there. These are people who are not promoting themselves. They share with each other and tend to serve the needs of others. They are very likely to offer a stability and grounding not found in other groups. They offer a place to grow-in-community.

Gabriel Marcel, the philosopher of personalism, says over and over in his writings that "the 'I' is the child of the we." Who are the people who make up the "we" for me? What is the effect on me of the people in my work environment? We cannot entirely control our companions or life situations, but we can edit from our lives the truly destructive elements. We do have some control over what we read, what we see in television and films, and the close friends we choose. Paul asks us to walk a tricky tightrope when he admonishes us to be in the world but not of it. One cannot be to the society what Jesus called "salt" if one does not participate in society. But what if we lose our saltiness? What good are we then, even to ourselves? Being a part of the world but not overinfluenced by it is a fine balance, one that calls for our full attention in constant daily decisions. Part of carrying out a daily life pattern directed toward the awareness of God is intentionally crafting one's formational environment.

Prayer

We have now discussed the ways in which work, study, and community can become integrated into a pattern of God-awareness, i.e., a rule of life. The feature most often associated with a rule, however, is that of prayer. We have already discussed several ways both to study about prayer and experience prayer. If prayer is to be incorporated in our lives, we must be especially realistic about what we are actually able to do.

How long can you realistically pray or keep holy silence in the morning? How long at night? To fit in with a demanding schedule, noon prayer may be only a moment in passing. People living with young family members face certain constraints; monks and nuns face others. Both monastic and family members live a life of boundaries, and each must consider what patterns are possible within those constraints. A crying baby or a carpool commute is a demanding constraint. So is making a living. I can only do what I can do. In making your own rule, try not to be overly ambitious. This will only set you up for discouragement and self-blame, should you not be able to carry out your intention. Start simply and with very modest goals. You can add to the pattern more successfully than subtract from it.

Morning prayer can be what you do with a cup of coffee, tea, or juice as you sit in a quiet place and before the household wakes. You may choose to read a short selection from one of the "sampler" books suggested previously, read another chapter or paragraph in a book, or meditate on the next psalm. (This is not reading of the study-type discussed in the previous chapter, but reading that prompts you to reflect in a prayerful way.) Quiet yourself before you begin the day, and ask God's guidance through it.

Noon is an ideal time to pray for the world and those in it for whom we especially care. The noonday sun shines on them as it does on us and reminds us of them.

Evening is a time to evaluate the day's events and our part in them. We may ask forgiveness for some wrong or neglect, thank God for the day's blessings and safety, and perhaps read a scripture passage or write in a journal.

Those wanting something handy and pocket-sized can order a little card called "Morning, Noon and Night Prayers" from Forward Movement Publications.[9] It gives written prayers and scripture for the three times of day.

Using the Rule in the Group

I suggest that each group member who chooses this discipline design a rule, or life pattern, for her own use. Refine it as you go along. Read the chapter on prayer, if you want some additional ideas in that regard. For your daily reading, you may want to look over the titles suggested in this book. To begin a study of the Benedictine rule, and for just sheer reading pleasure, read Kathleen Norris's popular book *The Cloister Walk.*[10] (Norris is also the author of *Dakota: A Spiritual Geography.*) If you are interested in learning more about Benedictine life, I suggest any of the writings of Esther de Waal.[11] If you are inclined to look further, I recommend *Saint Benedict for the Laity* by Eric Dean, a Presbyterian clergyman,[12] and *Spirituality for Everyday Living* by Brian Taylor.[13]

From time to time, as group members share their spiritual journeys with one another, they will exchange the experiments and experiences of living out their individual rules. Crafting a lifestyle designed for holding one's attention to a single end, the awareness of God, is a challenging project. This working out of a rule for one's daily life may be among the most creative and exciting enterprises that the group shares as they talk together.

As one part of their rule, the group may also choose to work together on some service project. Groups of this sort seldom sustain themselves without some "outflow" to make way for the further inflow of spirit. That is to say, we stop getting when we stop giving. You individually, or the group at large, may choose, as a part of your rule, to adopt a stretch of highway and pick up trash, deliver Meals-on-Wheels, tutor in a local school, take Communion to the home-bound, or any number of things. The group's chief purpose is not these activities, but without them a certain vitality is lost, and things can become too self-absorbed.

We seek financial planners to map our economic future, and trainers to design diet and exercise programs for our health. We may even hire consultants who, for the sake of our sanity, will come to our offices or homes and reorganize our desks and closets! How, then, can we also care for the deepest part of ourselves, our spiritual life? I suggest the creation of a rule, a daily pattern designed to ground us in remembrance of the holy. To balance this pattern, include work, study, prayer, and community. Yours will no longer be a life of random drift or pointless activity. It will be an intentional life, the very best kind!

CHAPTER 8

Safeguards

> *Dialogue is an encounter between people, mediated by the world*
> *in order to name the world.*
>
> Paulo Freire

You have decided to start a spiritual formation group, and you want to be
sure all goes well, right from the start. This is important business, and
you suspect that there will be those who, doubting the value of something unfamiliar, will be watching to see how things go. Take out some
insurance. Here are some of the things you can do to lay the groundwork
for a good beginning.

Nuts and Bolts

It sounds trivial, but where and when to meet is important, even in a
group focused on spirituality. Many worthwhile enterprises have gone
down the tube because participants found the arrangements inconvenient
or psychologically uncomfortable. The most hospitable place, of course,
is someone's home. Whether you always meet at one particular home or
rotate among several homes doesn't matter as long as everyone can find
the place and comfortably get there. If a home is not convenient, choose
a room in a church or counseling center that seats only a few more than
the number expected. Avoid seating group members in an area where, as
they try to pray or present their studies and stories, they can see or hear
passersby

   Begin on time. End on time. Those who want to linger may do so,
but those with baby sitters or other commitments want to know they can

depend on the schedule. If coffee or tea is convenient, that is nice. Occasionally someone may bring cookies, but note that eating food takes time, and there is little enough time scheduled here for all there is to do. If the group members had wanted a major social event, they could have chosen any of the many other activities available. They likely chose this group for deeply felt reasons, so stick with the intention!

It was suggested at the outset that a two-hour session is a workable format. The first two or three meetings may be held weekly, just to get off to a solid start. If the group chooses later to continue meeting less often, fine. Whatever works! The group can be ongoing and open-ended, or it can be time limited. You might try committing for about six to nine months and see what the members then decide regarding continuing. Beginning with a time limit will give those who later drop out, because of scheduled commitments, a chance to participate for the stated time. It is not a good idea for people to join and drop out randomly. It is likely that people will not see this sort of group as a "drop-in" setting, where they attend occasionally and miss most of the time. Those who learn what the group is about will probably commit for a sustained period, stopping only when they need to do so. The group will change over time, but that change is likely to be gradual.

Collegiality

Because the spiritual formation group is self-directing, you will want to thoroughly discuss and clear the project with whoever is in charge of activities in your church or counseling center. You need their support to make this project work. If you are the clergyperson or the director who approves such things, and you choose to make this a lay-led enterprise, I suggest you select a potential convener and ask that person to read this book. Ask for his or her personal response. Clergy, convener, and potential participants should have interest in beginning a group learning experience that is not a typical teacher-student arrangement, but rather a mutual enterprise shared among colleagues.

In the case of counseling centers, I cannot say too strongly that the spiritual formation group is for exploration and not for therapy. The counseling center is simply offering a well-planned structure to those clients wanting spiritual growth in a reliable setting. In the spiritual formation group, the center is offering opportunity for mutual mentoring, not supervised therapy for problem solving. Select as convener the staff member whose interests are in the spiritual growth area and who is able to transition from the role of mental health professional to facilitator—one among peers and fellow seekers. Experience in group work need not be as developed as that required for leading therapy groups because the spiritual formation group is based on a collegial rather than a training model. This leads us to wonder exactly what makes for good leadership in this kind of group, whatever the setting.

Choosing a Convener

The word *convener* may be the best choice for a group whose purpose is for members to learn from one another. *The person who convenes, or calls the group together, is not the teacher.* This is not a class, so to speak, with lectures, although different members will be presenting in areas they have studied. This is a meeting of people who want to experience greater closeness to God in their lives. The one who calls them together and who sees that things stay on track will need to be a person who understands this distinction.

Seasoned is the best word I can summon to describe what is needed in the convener. By this I mean one who has developed some patience with life and who knows there is much more to learn and experience. This is a person whose purpose is discovery; her agenda is not that members should agree to some particular view. It will help, of course, if the convener has some familiarity with Christian traditions, biblical material, and even theology. But openness is more important than information. Having a knowledgeable person is secondary to having one with a humble and questing spirit.

Look also for the ability to listen. People who are controllers usually cannot do this. What is needed is a convener who is, above all, curious. This person believes that everyone has something of value to bring to the mix and has the patience to wait for the gifts of each. This person listens not only for the voices of others, but for the voice of God. This man or woman may be less than expert in the spiritual journey, as are others in the group, but the essential skill lies in his ability to attend to both the audible words spoken by others and the quiet unspoken words of Spirit.

Do you need an organizer? Only to a degree. If organizing is not the convener's strength, he may want to ask someone who does this well to help with announcements, time-and-place arrangements, and meeting dates. The convener's chief functions are to see that the agreed upon time framework is kept, that the study chosen has a presenter ready for that meeting, and to keep the focus on spirituality. There will be no need for roll taking or the giving of certificates of completion. We are into an experience here, not an achievement.

Preventing Abuse

There are all kinds of motives for wanting to "be spiritual." You hope for the best and are forewarned about the rest. One person who can pose a problem is the *helper*. This is a well-meaning sort who wants only to make things better for everybody. During the time of sharing, for instance, someone will recount a tragedy or describe some adversity that has brought pain to her life. How could God let this happen? The helper-type tends to jump in and protest with something like, "Oh, you don't really feel that way!" or, "It's not so bad; I'm sure this will pass." The worst comment is "Be grateful! Just think how much more other people are suffering."

The abuse here is that the one telling about his pain has not been taken seriously, nor has he been truly listened to. Our pain must first be heard before it can be healed. The dragon must be named before it can be slain. It is difficult to blame so well intentioned a person as the helper, but see to it that those in your group who express pain are not discounted. They are in good company (Job and the psalmist), and God can bear their doubting, even their anger.

Another problem is posed by the *entertainer*. These people feel that the only merit they bring to a friendship is their knowledge of what goes on in the lives of others. Without intending to be malicious, they will tell friends outside the group those things that go on within the group that they believe will capture the attention of a listener, i.e., they will seek to entertain. Again, these people are usually not malicious, only insecure. The best defense is to remind the group regularly that confidentiality is essential. If you learn that what is private is being discussed outside the group, say something about it to the person who betrayed confidence. You can be loving about it, but also emphatic in saying that it not occur again, that respecting confidences is part of the group covenant. With this kind of person, it is important to mention the hurt that the breach brought to another. They were not thinking of that when they spoke. It may also be important to let entertainers know that they are valued for their legitimate efforts in the group, and not for their special inside knowledge about others.

And then there is the *devil's advocate*. Taken to the extreme, this person takes the opposite side of an issue, no matter what it is. Did you have a high spiritual moment? This person might counter, "You just had indigestion!" Have you come to some important insight? "Only fools still think like that!" Perhaps you are interested in a significant theological or social issue. "That's just fuzzy-headed thinking spawned by subversives." So how does one respond to such negativity? What the negative devil's advocate wants from you is an argument that will put him in the spotlight. Rather than defending your point, say how his comment affects you, or simply ignore it. Either way, you avoid escalating a no-win conflict by not allowing it to become a drama. Like the entertainer, the devil's advocate is not thinking about how this affects others. This may need to be explained, if it becomes a problem that interferes.

The person described above is the unpleasant version. Not all devil's advocates are problems. Some make a positive contribution by taking the opposing side in order to sharpen the thinking of the group. Just imagine that what you said actually is fuzzy thinking. Who better to put you back on the right track than a person with a sharp mind and good critical skills? This person's motive may not be negativity but clarity. The group just may benefit from the good version of this kind of person.

Finally, we have all known the *time blotter*. They take up all the allowed time with their own ramblings, stories, and comments. No one else has a chance to speak. Everyone wonders who will stop these people. If they are not stopped, the group will die. You might be amazed to know that many of these people are simply not aware of how they disenfranchise the rest. They become so engrossed in hearing their words that they have no idea they are blotting up the time. Most of them only need to have this pointed out in order to improve. Hints will not do, as they are unaware of trespassing. The convener can privately tell them exactly how many minutes are available for the group, and how many of those minutes were taken by them. Ask what they can do about the needs of the others to speak. They will figure it out. What you hope is that they will make their contributions in a more concise way and surprise everyone with their insights, once those can be appreciated.

Accountability

Earlier we talked about the danger of any group within the church becoming a lone-ranger operation, having no accountability to anyone. "A church within the church" is what some call it. When we engage the services of clergy, we expect them to be responsible for contributing to our spiritual health, and we would not like it if they paid no attention to movements and stirrings within the congregation. On the other hand, a lay-led spiritual growth group will become passive, and finally ineffective, if it allows the pastor or priest to "do it for them." What is needed is a balance between accountability and autonomy.

In stating that the spiritual formation group is best conceived as a lay-led project, I am not suggesting that a "No Clergy Allowed" sign be posted. We cannot possibly expect that any clergyperson can fulfill our mandate to "shepherd the flock" if she doesn't know what is going on within the flock. You will probably think of several ways your group can achieve a balance between involvement and distance. Here are four you may want to try.

First, the group can regularly invite a clergyperson to be its guest and can foster its spiritual growth by asking him to help in contributing to some of the study material in which the group is then engaged. Clergy may be invited to be study presenters on some occasions, or to serve as resource people in the discussion of the study. If pastors or priests wish to stay for the entire meeting time, they may be invited to do so, but not to lead the prayer or sharing time, unless that is specifically desired by the group. During the time of sharing, clergy might share their journeys with the group as fellow seekers, learning and growing. The benefits of this kind of interaction are great, for the guest clergy and the group. We learn to love and accept each other through truly knowing about the other. How nice to see one's pastor or priest, not as a role, but as a person! Clergy will also benefit by getting a feel for what is happening in the lives of those present. They may wish to actually join the group to nourish their own spiritual life. Because most clergy are natural leaders, there will be a temptation on the part of members to relinquish charge of the group to them. It must be clear that in this group, at least, every person is a peer member. If the clergyperson feels that something is going wrong in the group, that can most usefully be addressed by discussing it within the group. Asking nonthreatening questions is a good way to start.

A second suggestion for accountability is for the convener to consult, perhaps once a month, with the church clergy or with another staff person who is particularly interested in fostering spiritual growth. This is not just to report the actions of the group, but to discuss how better to encourage its growth. Above all else, this is a cooperative effort, not a competitive one to see who has control. One of the tasks of the staff consultant will be to encourage the convener to grow in her own spiritual life so that her participation with the group will be enhanced.

A third accountability safeguard is for the group to invite as a guest a spiritual director experienced with one-on-one work. Such a director will be fascinated with what you are doing and may be able to encourage areas of growth and point out possible pitfalls typical to the spiritual quest. Having a person outside the group meet with members brings an objective voice and an alternative point of view.

Finally, we are accountable to God. Within the group, this question should be asked regularly: "Are we becoming more like Jesus, or less like Jesus?" Another way of putting it is "Am I becoming more open to God in my life; am I less proud, more loving?" Once asked, the question deserves serious thought, and an answer.

Starting New Groups

Any well-bonded, growing, and excited group feels threatened when it is suggested that some in the group leave it to begin a new group. Nobody wants to break up "that good ole gang of ours." When a group grows to eight to ten members, it is time to do something. Some are inclined to put a time limit on how long a group can meet, and insist that groups be reorganized frequently. Unfortunately, this doesn't take into account the unique needs of any single group, and the strategy seldom works. I am indebted to Rev. Dick Wills, in Fort Lauderdale, for suggesting a solution that works for them. Wills says that his church went through a plateau, when groups did very well but were not duplicating themselves to make new opportunities for others. To remedy this, at the very beginning of a group, they enlisted two members who would commit to start a new group when the current group became too large. This built-in expectation of change, says Wills, got the work going again, and their use of groups continues to grow. Prof. Jon Rainbow of Southern Baptist Seminary in Louisville, an expert in group work, agrees that preparing for growth from the very beginning is essential. He suggests placing in each group a person who knows from the outset that he or she is training for beginning a new group. Rainbow tells me that once people become entrenched and comfortable, it is not possible to make change. "Stagnation is detrimental to spiritual growth," he says.

Allowing the Spirit Liberty

I suspect that many of us who say we trust God don't. We don't trust God to be capable of self-defense, to tolerate variety, or to bear our anger. We cannot bear it ourselves if what we do for God is a "failure." Will it be all right with you if you give your best effort, and your spiritual formation group doesn't make it? Does that mean that God is a failure, or simply that it may not be time for it now? We need to take the pressure off ourselves by giving the project permission to succeed or to fail. And would it be a failure, anyway, if what we want to happen is not what does happen?

My point is that we are not in charge of what actually occurs in the spiritual lives of others. God's Spirit is in charge of that. Our very important part is to provide a way for ourselves, and possibly others, to be more open to what God is doing among us. A spiritual formation group is simply a way to open avenues of access. By praying, studying, and sharing with each other, we make ourselves more available to what God may wish to accomplish.

Just as we give ourselves permission to "fail," so we must also give ourselves permission to succeed, or rather, for God to succeed in us. It may be that this group will be unlike any other of which we have ever been a part. What if, indeed, we do experience great growth in our spirituality and in our sense of God being with us? What if one member feels a strong inclination to do something she has never before considered doing? Or be something he has not imagined until now? In the face of such "success," one might be tempted to put on the brakes! When we said we would like to grow, we may not have taken into consideration whose definition of growth we were inviting. The Creator's idea of what we can become is so much larger than our own. It is like seeing a two-year-old and imagining the potential the child cannot even guess exists. Succeeding in things spiritual begs for the spirit of adventure. I've heard Bishop Stewart Zabriskie, of the Episcopal Diocese of Nevada, quoted as saying that there are trips, journeys, pilgrimages, and adventures, but only in adventures is the destination unknown. In some sense, the spiritual quest is all of these. In the first three we know our destination to be God. The adventure, however, is different. In an adventure we do not know ahead of time all the riches to which our quest will lead, and the new paths down which we will go. We need safeguards for the journey, but to have an adventure, we must not be *too* safe.

CHAPTER 9

Commencement

In spiritual practice . . .the goal is always the recovery of wholeness.

Thomas Matus

By now you may suspect that what is presented here is not another church activity designed simply to fill the spring or fall schedule of events. A spiritual formation group, if it fulfills its long-term purpose, enables the quest for nearness to God. The group's intent is to connect with that nutrient source desperately needed by what Elton Trueblood called "the cut flower generation." Spiritual resources rooted in individual lives underpin any authentic flowering of religion. Without that spirituality that nourishes, first the activities and then the structures of organized worship begin to wilt. There is no longer any good reason for either. It is embarrassing when church leaders must try as hard as they do to make a case for the worship of God. Something is missing here.

A Call to Competence

In a society of specialists, we allow others to do for us what we once did for ourselves. Given the complicated nature of some fields of endeavor, such as computer repair or financial management, that is not a bad idea. We need the expertise of those trained in what we do not do. Tragically, we have also handed over our spiritual lives to "experts." The experts are not thrilled about this. These are the theologically trained clergy and church staff who see that the power we have given them is often counter-productive. It is slowly making the church powerless! The picture that comes to mind is that of a see-saw. A single person, the expert, sits on one end and a congregation on the other; how effectively can the one pump for the many? Clergy often report a psychological exhaustion that sets in midway through their ministry—when they begin to grasp the difficulty of being the spiritual stand-in for the impoverished lives of others. It is too much.

But it is not the clergy who suffer most. Many laypeople know what it is like to enter crisis and have no inner resources. Many know the panic of losing a job, from downsizing or retirement, and discovering they have no identity other than as a worker. And the death of a contemporary always stirs up anxiety when we don't know what we think about God's reality. It is not difficult to argue that human life without spiritual content is too hard to manage.

As laypeople we must become competent in our own spiritual development. This is not someone else's job. If I do not care for myself, who is supposed to do that? I believe that there is such a thing as *the stewardship of the self.* Church members place great emphasis on the stewardship of money, energy, time, and anything else the church needs. We place almost no emphasis on our spiritual development, that feature of our lives that gives meaning and impetus to all the rest.

Breaking New Ground

Admittedly, this attention to the spiritual is breaking new ground for some. Others are fortunate to have learned to attend to the inner life. If an emphasis on spirituality has not been characteristic of your church's programmatic offerings, you may be hard pressed to make a case for it. The need for deepened spiritual life is not quickly explained, as is the justification for a group studying other worthy topics such as Where My Mission Dollar Goes or Outreach Opportunities. (It could be pointed out that mission and outreach dry up when people do.) But people are so accustomed to running on empty that the argument for a deepened spirituality may not make sense to them. If a way to foster spiritual growth in your congregation is what you want, you will first need to gather support. It may take a little educating of others on your part to show how important the enterprise is.

The Group Begins

Let's say you are interested in beginning a spiritual formation group. How do you find members? How will the group be maintained? And what can you expect from it?

Finding Members

It is great to see large numbers of people show up, revealing interest in their spiritual growth. Such wonders have happened. More likely, you can expect to start with three or four seekers. Does that sound like too few? Not necessarily. Remember what you are after. This is a group whose purpose is depth, not popularity.

To find people interested in such a venture, describe what the group will be about. Because that is somewhat difficult to do, you may want to carefully word a bulletin insert that can be distributed in your church (or a folded flyer made available to clients, if you are in a counseling center). Describe the group as a regular gathering of those who are particularly interested in growing in the spiritual disciplines of prayer and study of spiritual experience. Say that a specific plan will be followed (this book). Provide a telephone number so that anyone interested can call and talk to someone who will discuss this further. Unlike a churchwide campaign, which is promoted in headlines and at every speaking opportunity, this project is more personal. Once the initial announcement is made, it is essentially a word-of-mouth approach, The most successful groups seem to be those whose members were personally invited by someone interested in starting the group. Invite people based on their interest in things spiritual. An additional consideration, though not nearly so important, may be that participants share something in common, for instance, being single or in families or mothers or perhaps just that they live in the same zip code and can easily get to one another's houses.

Maintaining the Group

How will the group be maintained? The spiritual formation group is maintained only insofar as it meets the spiritual needs of members. In other words, it stands or falls as it either serves its purpose or does not. This prompts us to wonder if we are the ones responsible for making things work. Wasn't it said earlier that God's Spirit is in charge? If so, then how can we ensure that the group serves its purpose, and thus survives?

Our task is to foster openness to God. We will always need to wonder if what we do is accomplishing that, and we will never know with certainty. But we can make some pretty safe assumptions. By disciplining ourselves to pray and listen, we consent to hear God's voice. By promoting the study of religious inquiry and the spiritual lives of others, we open the possibilities of imagination, making it possible for God to work with us in new ways. By committing to share with one another our spiritual journeys, we grow together, allowing God to reach us through community. It is not that God is helpless to come to us. Rather, it is our part to open ourselves to the God who is already here. A group is maintained by its intentional openness in responding to God.

What Can We Expect?

I don't mean to be deliberately enigmatic, but what we can expect is the unexpected. This sounds a bit scary, at first hearing, but the issue is really whether we feel we can trust God with ourselves. We assure others that they can "trust God," but when it comes to letting go of our own agenda long enough to seek God's, it is different for us. What if we don't like what we learn? You can always back out, you know. Above all, God is not coercive. It is the chief part of love to respect the self-hood of another, and we will not be forced into any unwilling compli-ance. But what if I learn that God's love for me enriches my life, open-ing up paths that are exciting, giving new meaning to each day? What we can expect from the group is an opportunity to find out.

We can also expect that if group participants begin to deepen their own spiritual lives, the life of the church will deepen as well. This does not happen within months; it is, like so many good things, slow and steady. An oven heats rapidly, but even a candle can warm the entire dish if you give it long enough. Authentic spirituality is permeating. The deep connection to God among members of the group will affect the life of the church in subtle but significant ways.

We spoke earlier of mission and outreach. There are, as we know, people who are better at action and doing than at contemplative stillness. It doesn't matter; both are needed. Some of the more action oriented will be in the spiritual growth group; others will not find it appealing. But all will benefit from the influence of the few. There may even be some who, at last, find something they can do for God other than get busier. We can expect from the group, if it fulfills its purpose, an enrichment of personal life, an uplift in church spirituality, and an increased reason for its outreach efforts.

Attending to Aftercare

Much as you wish otherwise, there will be some who will join and then leave the group. It is difficult to have shared much and then to separate. We do not like having our worlds disrupted. But someone is transferred, another has night meetings that conflict, and another loses interest. Do not allow any of these to drift from your care. Follow up, not so that they will "come back," but because you know and care about them.

Stay in Touch

People who move away will be faced with the task of finding a place of spiritual growth in their new communities. As they search, they will need the encouragement they get in hearing from members of the group.

People who drop out because obligations keep them from meetings will gradually feel out of the loop, cut off from this opportunity to find the "something more" they hoped for. Keep them updated on what is happening, and let them have access to what is being read and discussed. Those conflicting meetings may not go on forever. Tell them they remain in your prayers.

Inevitably, someone loses interest. Did we fail to meet her needs, or were we not affirming enough? Probably not. That person simply may not be at a life juncture where this sort of experience makes sense. But stay in touch, occasionally relating what the group is talking about to allow for a point of reentry. This is not done to seduce the person back or to inflict guilt. Occasional contact is made so that she may comfortably choose what she needs as life unfolds. We do not know what particular people may need and can't control what they choose. Our task is to make the choice possible.

Encourage Continuity

Those who have stayed with the group for a while may have developed a personal daily pattern or rule. Should someone leave the group for any reason, encourage him to continue in prayer and study. Send any papers, book titles, or new information you have on the subject of daily prayer, so he can keep up with new things the group learns. And do ask him to stay in touch with you, sharing valuable experiences with the group. Occasional calls or letters to and from the group members furnish new perspectives and provide grounding in the faith community.

Seek Individual Direction

The person changing location will no doubt have a hard time finding a group dedicated to spiritual development. If such a search is not successful and this person is not able to start a group, encourage her to seek individual spiritual direction. Detective work may be necessary to find a director. Suggest inquiring at a local seminary, if there is one, talking to a pastor, priest, or the director of a pastoral counseling center, or calling the local diocesan office of the Roman Catholic or Episcopal Churches. Spiritual direction or spiritual friendship, as some prefer to call it, is a marvelous way to grow, and one gets the undivided attention of the director whose task it is to foster that growth. Of course, as in anything else, it depends on the competence of the person doing the directing, so be a shopper. It is not inappropriate to ask about a person's training, theological and otherwise, and about her experience in working with directees. After all, this is one's inmost self we are talking about. It is at least as important as finding a good physician.

The Role of the Church

It is unfortunate that anyone should have to do detective work to find resources for spiritual growth. The church is the place, the very place, where the spiritual life should be fostered, indeed, focused upon. We should expect to find resources there. It is not enough to tell someone to "get active" in the local church, as valuable as that is for the member and the newcomer. It is not enough.

I trust that what is offered here as a plan for fostering spiritual growth will be part of the answer for congregations that see their task as that of reconciliation. In human interactions we are reconciled to one another, first by personal contact, then by learning to hear the other, and finally, by being willing to speak the truth. We are reconciled to God in exactly the same way: As we pray, we make contact; as we study we learn to listen to the voice of God and others who tell of God; as we share, we become willing to speak the truth about our lives and God's interaction with us. These are the three tasks proposed for the spiritual formation group.

There is no need to wonder what the will of God is for us. God's will is that we flourish! We do this by becoming whole, which is to say, being fully what we are created to be. Only the Creator can accomplish this within us. It is time to make deeper connections to the nutrient Source.

NOTES

Preface
1. Nancy T. Ammerman, *Congregation and Community:Stability and Change in American Religion* (Newark, NJ: Rutgers University Press, 1996).

Chapter 1
1. Karen Armstrong, *A History of God: The 4000-Year Quest of Judaism, Christianity and Islam* (New York: Alfred A. Knopf, 1993), 4. Used with permission of the publisher.
2. Ibid., p.xxi.
3. Gustavo Gutierrez, *We Drink from Our Own Wells* (Maryknoll, NY: Orbis Books, 1984), 35.
4. *Trinity News*, Trinity Church, 74 Trinity Pl., New York, NY 10006, 1996.
5. Cited in Russell Levenson, Jr., "Interview with the Reverend Dr. John R. W. Stott," *Anglican Digest* (Transfiguration, 1996), 37.

Chapter 2
1. Adolf Harnack as quoted in Michael Cox, *Handbook of Christian Spirituality: A Guide to Figures and Teaching from the Biblical Era to the Twentieth Century* (San Francisco: Harper & Row, 1983), 42.
2. Kenneth Leech, *Soul Friend: The Practice of Christian Spirituality* (San Francisco: Harper & Row, 1977).
3. Dick Wills, "Lay Pastors: The Door to a New Future," *Circuit Rider* (April 1995), 9-11.
4. Hans H. Breuer, *Recovery: Group Leader Training Manual, 1995* and *Small Group Leader Training*, Vineyard Community Church, 1391

E. Crescentville Rd. , Cincinnati, OH 45246; phone (513) 671-0422.
Describe your intended use and ask which of these two manuals best
meets your needs.

5. Leech, *Soul Friend*, 87.

6. Susan Howatch, *Glittering Images* (New York: Fawcett Crest,
1987). This title is the first in a series of six novels set in midtwentieth-
century England. This citation is for the paperback version.

7. Alvin Toffler, "Cyberspace and Society" (Paper delivered to The
Progress and Freedom Foundation, Aspen, CO, 1996).

8. Tilden Edwards, *Living in the Presence: Disciplines for the
Spiritual Heart* (San Francisco: Harper & Row, 1987).

9. Marjorie J. Thompson, *Soul Feast: An Invitation to the Christian
Spiritual Life* (Louisville: Westminster/John Knox, 1995).

10. Gerald May, *Pilgrimage Home: The Conduct of Contemplative
Practice in Groups* (New York: Paulist Press, 1979).

Chapter 3

1. Ibid., 21.

Chapter 4

1. Rudolf Otto, *The Idea of the Holy* (New York: Oxford University
Press, 1958).

2. Desmond Tutu, ed., *An African Prayer Book* (New York: Doubleday, 1995), 11.

3. Augustine, *Confessions X*, trans. R. S. Pine-Coffin (Harmondsworth.
England: Penguin, 1967), 27.

4. Robert Wood, *A Thirty-Day Experiment in Prayer* (Nashville: The
Upper Room, 1978).

5. *The Book of Common Prayer* (New York: The Church Hymnal
Corporation, 1979), 219.

6. Frank C. Laubach, *Prayer: The Mightiest Force in the World*
(New York: Fleming H. Revell, 1946), 56.

7. Ann and Barry Ulanov, *Primary Speech: A Psychology of Prayer*
(Atlanta: John Knox, 1982), 3.

8. Mike Samuels and Nancy Samuels, *Seeing with the Mind's Eye*
(New York: Random House, 1975).

9. Rachel Naomi Remen, "Wholeness," in *Healing and the Mind*, ed.
Bill Moyers (New York: Doubleday, 1993), 347.

10. Ulanov, *Primary Speech*, 3.

11. *The Way of a Pilgrim* and *The Pilgrim Continues His Way*, trans. R. M. French (New York: Seabury, 1965).

12. Aryeh Kaplan, *Jewish Meditation: A Practical Guide* (New York: Schocken Books, 1985), 56.

13. Ulanov, *Primary Speech,* 18.

14. Basil Pennington, *Centering Prayer* (Garden City, NY: Doubleday, 1980).

15. Thomas Keating, *Intimacy with God* (New York: Crossroad, 1995).

16. Thomas Keating, *Spiritual Journey* videotape series, 1987. Address inquiries to Contemporary Communication, 7 Mesa Ln., Colorado Springs, CO 80906. Att.: Walter Lawson; phone (719) 632-7320.

17. Keating, *Intimacy with God*, 64. Used with permission of the publisher.

18. Gay Hendricks, *Conscious Breathing: Breathwork for Health, Stress Release, and Personal Mastery* (New York: Bantam Books, 1995).

19. Nancy Roth, *The Breath of God: An Approach to Prayer* (Cambridge, MA: Cowley, 1990).

20. Ron DelBene, with Mary and Herb Montgomery, *The Breath of Life: A Simple Way to Pray* (Minneapolis: Winston Press, 1981).

21. Thomas Keating quoted in Kenneth Woodward, et al., "Talking to God," *Newsweek* (January 6, 1992), 44.

22. Oswald Chambers, *My Utmost for His Highest* (New York: Dodd Mead, 1935), 210.

23. Viktor Frankl quoted in Larry Dossy, *Healing Words: The Power of Words and the Practice of Medicine* (San Francisco: HarperSanFrancisco, 1993), 13.

24. Dossy, *Healing Words*, 24.

25. E. Glenn Hinson, *A Serious Call to a Contemplative Life-Style* (Philadelphia: Westminster, 1974), ch. 4.

26. Susan Ertz quoted in "Sunbeams," *The Sun* 196 (March 1992): 40.

27. Caroline Myss, *Anatomy of the Spirit: The Seven Stages of Power and Healing* (New York: Harmony Books, 1996), 282.

Chapter 5

1. Steel's Used Christian Books, 3827 Independence Ave., Kansas City, MO, 64124; phone (816) 483-2004; fax (816) 483-2448.

Kregel's Bookstore, P.O. Box 2607, Grand Rapids, MI 49501-2607; phone (616) 459-9444; toll-free fax (888) 873-2665.

Stevens Book Shop, 7109, Old Wake Forest Rd., Raleigh, NC 27616; phone (919) 872-5995.

Powell's City of Books, 1005 W. Burnside, Portland, OR 97209; phone (800) 878-READ.

Baker Book House, P.O. Box 6287, Grand Rapids, MI 49546; phone (616) 957-3110; fax (616) 957-0965.

Ex Libris Theological Books, P.O. Box 810, Oak Lawn, IL 60454-0810; phone (312) 955-3456; fax (312) 955-4116. (The store is located at 1340 E. 55th in Chicago.) Specializes in academic religious titles.

Archives Bookshop, 1387 E. Washington Blvd., Pasadena, CA 91104; phone (818) 797-4756; fax (818) 797-5237. Specializes in academic religious titles.

2. C. S. Lewis, *The Screwtape Letters* (New York: Harcourt Brace Jovanovich, 1958).

3. Rueben P. Job and Norman Shawchuck, eds., *A Guide to Prayer for Ministers and Other Servants* (Nashville: The Upper Room, 1983).

4. Rueben P. Job and Norman Shawchuck, eds., *A Guide to Prayer for All God's People* (Nashville: The Upper Room, 1990).

5. Roger Pooley and Philip Seddon, eds., *The Lord of the Journey: A Reader in Christian Spirituality* (London: Collins, 1986).

6. John W. Doberstein, ed., *Minister's Prayer Book: An Order of Prayers and Readings* (Philadelphia: Fortress Press, 1959).

7. Oswald Chambers, *My Utmost for His Highest* (Uhrichsville, Ohio: Barbour and Co., 1963). (First published in 1935 by Dodd Mead.)

8. Frederick Buechner, *Listening to Your Life: Daily Meditations with Frederick Buechner*, George Conner, comp. (San Francisco: HarperSanFrancisco, 1992).

9. Urban T. Holmes, *A History of Christian Spirituality: An Analytical Introduction* (San Francisco: Harper & Row, 1980).

10. The Anglican Bibliopole, 858 Church St., Saratoga Springs, NY 12866-8615; phone (518) 587-7470.

11. John J. O'Meara, ed., *An Augustine Reader* (Garden City, NY: Doubleday, Image 1973).

12. Carol Lee Flinders, *Enduring Grace: Living Portraits of Seven Woman Mystics* (San Francisco: HarperSanFrancisco, 1993).

13. Francis of Assisi, *The Little Flowers of St. Francis of Assisi* (New York: Book of the Month Club, 1996).

14. Matthew Fox, commentator, *Breakthrough: Meister Eckhart's Creation Spirituality in New Translation* (Garden City, NY: Doubleday, Image, 1980).

15. John Woolman, *The Journal and Major Essays of John Woolman*, ed. Phillips P. Moulton (New York: Oxford University Press, 1971).

16. Evelyn Underhill, *The Spiritual Life* (New York: Harper & Row, Harper Devotional Classics, 1937); *Mysticism* (New York: Harper & Row, 1993).

17. Thomas R. Kelly, *A Testament of Devotion* (New York: Harper & Row, 1941).

18. Dag Hammarskjold, *Markings* (New York: Alfred A. Knopf, 1964).

19. Thomas Merton, *No Man Is an Island* (San Diego: Harcourt Brace Jovanovich, 1955).

20. Henri J. M. Nouwen, *The Genesee Diary: Report from a Trappist Monastery* (Garden City, NY: Doubleday, 1976).

21. Richard Foster, *Celebration of Discipline: The Path to Spiritual Growth* (San Francisco: Harper & Row, 1978).

22. David Keirsey and Marilyn Bates, *Please Understand Me: Character and Temperament Types* (Del Mar, CA: Prometheus Nemesis, 1984).

23. Chester P. Michael and Marie C. Norrisey, *Prayer and Temperament: Different Prayer Forms for Different Personality Types* (Charlottesville, VA: The Open Door, 1984).

24. Isabel Briggs Myers, *Gifts Differing* (Palo Alto, CA: Consulting Psychologists Press, 1985).

25. James W. Fowler, *Stages of Faith: The Psychology of Human Development and the Quest for Meaning* (San Francisco: Harper & Row, 1981).

26. Carol Gilligan, *In a Different Voice: Psychological Theory and Women's Development* (Cambridge, MA: Harvard University Press, 1982).

27. Robert Kegan, *The Evolving Person: Problems and Process in*

Human Development (Cambridge, MA: Harvard University Press, 1982).

28. Scott Peck, *Further along the Road Less Traveled* (New York: Simon & Schuster, 1993), ch. 7.

29. Gail Sheehy, *New Passages: Mapping Your Life across Time* (New York: Random House, 1995).

30. Daniel A. Helminiak, *Spiritual Development: An Interdisciplinary Study* (Chicago: Loyola University Press, 1987).

31. Erik H. Erikson, *Childhood and Society* (New York: W. W. Norton, 1963).

32. Corinne Ware, *Discover Your Spiritual Type: A Guide to Individual and Congregational Growth* (Bethesda, MD: The Alban Institute, 1995). To order call 1-800-486-1318.

33. St. Ignatius of Loyola, *The Spiritual Exercises of St. Ignatius*, trans. Anthony Mettola (Garden City, NY: Doubleday, Image, 1964).

34. James W. Skehan, *Place Me with Your Son: Ignatian Spirituality in Everyday Life*, 3rd. ed. (Washington, DC: Georgetown University Press, 1991). To use this book effectively, the reader will need a copy of *The Spiritual Exercises of St. Ignatius* that delineates Ignatius' numbered paragraphs.

35. Michael and Norrisey, *Prayer and Temperament*.

36. Ware, *Discover Your Spiritual Type*.

37. Huston Smith, *The Illustrated World's Religions: A Guide to Our Wisdom Traditions* (San Francisco: HarperSanFrancisco, 1994).

38. Milton Steinberg, *Basic Judaism* (San Diego: Harcourt Brace Jovanovich, Harvest Book, 1975).

39. Abraham Joshua Heschel, *God in Search of Man: A Philosophy of Judaism* (New York: Farrar, Straus and Giroux, 1955, 1985).

40. Arthur J. Magida, ed., *How to Be a Perfect Stranger*, (Woodstock, VT: Jewish Lights, 1996).

41. James F. White, *Protestant Worship: Traditions in Transition* (Louisville, KY: Westminster/John Knox, 1989).

42. Frank S. Mead, revised by Samuel Hill, *Handbook of Denominations in the United States,* 10th ed. (Nashville: Abingdon,1990).

43. Alfred McBride, *Essentials of the Faith: A Guide to the Catechism of the Catholic Church* (Huntington, IN: Our Sunday Visitor, 1994).

44. Kevin Orlin Johnson, *Why Do Catholics Do That?* (New York: Random House, Ballantine, 1995).

45. Thomas Bokenkotter, *A Concise History of the Catholic Church*, rev. ed. (Garden City, NY: Doubleday, Image, 1979).

46. Martin Luther, *The Small Catechism* (St. Louis, MO: Concordia, 1960).

47. Howard L. Rice, *Reformed Spirituality: An Introduction for Believers* (Louisville, KY: Westminster/John Knox, 1991), 139.

48. Frank C. Senn, ed., *Protestant Spiritual Traditions* (New York: Paulist Press, 1986).

49. Dietrich Bonhoeffer, *The Cost of Discipleship* (New York: Macmillan, 1963).

50. Urban T. Holmes, *What Is Anglicanism?* (Wilton, CT: Morehouse-Barlow, 1982).

51. Robert E. Webber, *Evangelicals on the Canterbury Trail: Why Evangelicals Are Attracted to the Liturgical Church* (Waco, TX: Word Books, 1985).

52. John Booty, *What Makes Us Episcopalians* (New York: Morehouse, 1982).

53. Corinne Ware, *What Is Liturgy?* (Cincinnati: Forward Movement, 1996). To order call 1-800-543-1813.

54. Kallistos Ware, *The Orthodox Way* (Crestwood, NY: St. Vladimir's Seminary Press, 1986).

55. Alexander Schmemann, *For the Life of the World: Sacraments and Orthodoxy* (Crestwood, NY: St. Vladimir's Seminary Press, 1988).

56. David Lowes Watson, "Methodist Spirituality," in *Protestant Spiritual Traditions*, ed. Frank C. Senn (New York: Paulist Press, 1986), 217.

57. Frank Whaling, *John and Charles Wesley: Selected Writings and Hymns* (New York: Paulist Press, 1981).

58. Branson L. Thurston, *The United Methodist Way* (Nashville: The Upper Room).

59. Kenneth L. Carder, *Living Our Beliefs: The United Methodist Way* (Nashville: Cokesbury, 1996).

60. Peter J. Paris, *The Spirituality of African American Peoples* (Minneapolis: Augsburg Fortress, 1994).

61. Howard Thurman, *Deep River and Negro Spirituality* (Richmond, IN: Friends United, 1975).

62. Southern Baptist Historical Society, Oklahoma Baptist University, P.O. Box 61838, Shawnee, OK 74810; phone (800) 966-2278.

63. Brooks Hayes and John E. Steely, *The Baptist Way of Life* (Macon, GA: Mercer University Press, 1993).

64. Robert G. Torbet, *A History of the Baptists* (Valley Forge, PA: Judson, 1963).

65. George M. Marsden, *Understanding Fundamentalism and Evangelicalism* (Grand Rapids: Eerdmans, 1991).

66. Elizabeth A. Johnson, *She Who Is: The Mystery of God in Feminist Theological Discourse* (New York: Crossroad, 1994).

67. Letty M. Russell and J. Shannon Clarkson, eds., *Dictionary of Feminist Theologies* (Louisville: Westminster/John Knox, 1996).

68. Linwood Urban, *A Short History of Christian Thought*, rev. ed. (New York: Oxford University Press, 1995).

Chapter 6

1. William H. Friedman, *How to Do Groups*, 2nd ed. (Northvale, NJ: Jason Aronson, 1994).

2. Robert J. Lovinger, *Working with Religious Issues in Therapy* (New York: Jason Aronson, 1984), 89.

3. Steven A. Beebe and John T. Masterson, *Communicating in Small Groups: Principles and Practices*, 3rd ed. (New York: HarperCollins, 1989), 51.

4. I have been unable to track down the author of this paraphrase, which I jotted down—but did not properly cite—in my reading.

Chapter 7

1. Claude E. Payne, "My Rule of Life," *The Texas Episcopalian* 99, no. 6 (June 1996): 2.

2. Umphrey Lee, *John Wesley and Modern Religion* (Nashville: Cokesbury, 1936).

3. Marion J. Hatchett, *Commentary on the American Prayer Book* (Minneapolis: Seabury, 1980), 89.

4. Robert Taft, *The Liturgy of the Hours in East and West*, 2nd rev. ed. (Collegeville, MN: Liturgical Press, 1993). This is a reliable history of how the hours of devotion developed.

5. Brother Lawrence, *The Practice of the Presence of God* (Old Tappan, NJ: Fleming H. Revell, Spire, 1977).

6. The Religious Book Club, P.O. Box 7000, Peabody, MA 01961-7000; phone (518) 977-5000.

7. Cokesbury, 201 Eighth Ave. South, P.O. Box 801, Nashville, TN 37202-0801; phone (800) 672-1789.

8. In addition to The Alban Institute, these three publishers have good catalogs featuring their own religious books: HarperSanFrancisco publishes Harper's Torch Letter Catalog, 1160 Battery St., San Francisco, CA 94111-1213; phone (800) 331-3761. Cowley Publications Catalog, 28 Temple Pl., Boston, MA 02111; phone (800) 225-1534; fax (617) 423-2354. Oxford University Press Religion Catalog, 198 Madison Ave., New York, NY 10016; phone (800) 451-7556; fax (919) 677-1303.

9. "Morning, Noon and Night Prayers," Forward Movement Publications, 412 Sycamore St., Cincinnati, OH 45202. This is a glossy 3 1/2 by 5 1/2 two-fold card. Also available as a card is "Praying the Hours" for those who wish to follow the eight hours of traditional monasticism.

10. Kathleen Norris, *The Cloister Walk* (New York: Riverhead Books, 1996).

11. Esther de Waal, *Seeking God: The Way of St. Benedict* (Collegeville, MN: Liturgical Press, 1985); *A Life-Giving Way* (Collegeville, MN: Liturgical Press, 1995). de Waal's second book does not include Benedict's rule in the text, so you will need to order the free booklet offered with the book. To order the booklet independently write to Liturgical Press, The Order of St. Benedict, Collegeville, MN 56321, and request *RB 1980: The Rule of St. Benedict* (1981).

12. Eric Dean, *Saint Benedict for the Laity* (Collegeville, MN: Liturgical Press, 1989).

13. Brian Taylor, *Spirituality for Everyday Living: An Adaption of the Rule of St. Benedict* (Collegeville, MN: Liturgical Press, 1989).